Introduction

Every day the news media scream out the fact that crisis is a way of life for human beings! One cannot listen to the news or read the news and remain unaware of the frequency and intensity of increasing crises over our nation and indeed, across the world. Every day, in this great land, tens of thousands of crises occur in diverse ways and with grievous consequences. The statistical evidence blares out the fact that the nation is in crisis.

On the average day in the U.S. thousands of children run away from home. Thousands of marriages end up in divorce. Thousands of illegitimate children are born. Thousands of abortions are performed, thousands of people enter into the valley of depression. Thousands contract one disease or another, thousands become intoxicated with alcohol. Thousands ingest illegal drugs, and hundreds attempt suicide. It should be obvious that the enormity of the crisis is horrendous. If I examine the statistics on a worldwide scale then these thousands become millions. Thus it is statistically accurate to state that every day millions of crises occur.

The occurrence of crises is a historical fact and an ever-increasing current reality. Perhaps, the urgency of addressing the matter of crisis prevention is brought out by a historical examination of the Great Depression. It was on October 24, 1929 that the complete collapse of the stock market began. Then on Tuesday, October 29th – known as Black Tuesday – the stock market really crashed leaving financial ruin and panic in its wake. This crash turned out to be a major crisis event in terms of its financial, social, psychological, emotional and spiritual consequences. In fact, in 1931 alone more than 20,000 Americans committed suicide as a result of this crisis event. Such statistics cannot really capture the magnitude of the crisis in all its negative dimensions. One must

1

understand that when 20,000 people commit suicide there remain hundreds of thousands who must deal with the crisis of losing a family member or friend because of the suicide. Only God knows the full extent of the impact of the Great Depression.

Since the late 1980's the annual number of suicides in the USA has averaged about 50,000. This is not just a cold figure. This represents the death of goals and dreams of whole families, of fathers and mothers, of children and grandchildren. The fact of suicide at such a rate proves that crisis events are part of life and that a significant percentage of the population are inadequately prepared to effectively deal with such crises.

Additionally, when we consider the alarming statistics concerning alcoholism and drug addiction and other such self-destructive addictions we are faced with a major problem that needs attention. In spite of the best intentions by government and other social agencies the use of drugs and alcohol continues to be a major crisis. A recent article in a leading newspaper presents us with frightening trends concerning the use of drugs. Concerning the use of heroin, the article says, *"According to treatment centers, hospital emergency rooms, law enforcement officials and heroin experts, the problem is growing. Although the overall numbers are small, the latest national survey shows that heroin use among teenagers has more then doubled since 1991. Our clinics are bursting at the seams"*.

Within recent times we have been witnessing an escalation of teen violence in the schools. What a frightening and shocking thing it is when a six year old school child murders another six year old with a gun as happened in the Michigan in February 2000. And none will soon forget that horrific day, April 20th 1999 when two teenage students at Columbine High School in Littleton, Colorado opened fire at fellow students. At the end of the shooting twelve students and a teacher lay dead, twenty-three wounded. The two teens killed themselves. This tragedy shocked the consciences of Americans from "sea to shining sea". Religious and secular authorities

2

WHOLENESS
&
HOLINESS

A Guide to minimize crisis
&
maximize your life for God

Dr. Lincoln A. Jailal

Printed in the United States by
Morris Publishing
3212 East Highway 30
Kearney, NE 68847
1-800-650-7888

This

Book

Is dedicated to

All those fearless servants of God

Who deny themselves.

Take up the cross of Jesus

And follow Him

Without fear of this culture

Because they desire to become

Whole and Holy in Jesus Christ Only!

WHOLENESS & HOLINESS
BY
Dr. Lincoln A. Jailal

A book dedicated to
supernatural healing and
changes in a person's life under
the Lord's control and the
acceptance of Him as the one
and only personal savior.

The occurrence of crises is a
historical fact and an ever-
increasing current reality. The
purpose of this book is to
educate and motivate people,
especially counselors, pastors
and parents, to practice and
teach a lifestyle that is able to
successfully minimize crisis
events and dysfunctional
responses to crisis events.

Contents

across the nation were quick to pontificate on this carnage but lamentably, the real causes of such a crisis have not yet been addressed. I do not wish to be a harbinger of evil news but I believe that this type of crisis will only worsen as our nation increases its distance from God and His laws of holiness.

The really tragic aspect of all of this is that it does not have to happen. Suicide, alcoholism, drug addiction and violence within the schools are responses to crises in the lives of people. These are external symptoms of much deeper problems within the human heart. Such dysfunctional responses are avoidable. In other words, much of the human suffering in our society need not happen. Some crises are definitely preventable! And certainly, self destructive crisis responses to crisis events are preventable.

Most adults grew up with the proverb; "An ounce of prevention is worth a pound of cure". This gem of wisdom is as true today as it ever was. Why should people waste time and money and energy finding a cure when they could have actually prevented the problem from occurring? The Holy Bible is a book full of wisdom. The problem is that even though most Americans own several copies of this book only a minority actually uses it as a guide to living.

In the book of Proverbs we discover numerous gems of wisdom, which, if diligently heeded can save humanity the majority of crises. We are told that, *"he who ignores discipline comes to poverty and shame, but whoever heeds correction is honored"* (Proverbs 13:18). In verse 20 of the same chapter God admonishes us that, *"he who walks with the wise grows wise but a companion of fools suffers harm."* In fact, throughout this book we find remarkable pieces of wisdom that make the case for prevention. Particularly insightful is this piece in Proverbs 14:15-17: *"A simple man believes anything, but a prudent man gives thought to his steps. A wise man fears the Lord but a fool is hotheaded and reckless. A quick tempered man does foolish things and a crafty man is hated."*

The purpose of this book is to educate and motivate people, especially counselors, pastors and parents, to practice and teach a lifestyle that can successfully minimize crisis events and dysfunctional responses to crisis events. I believe that far too little emphasis is placed on crisis minimization as a lifestyle. Too often, people, Christians included, engage in self-destructive behaviors that lead to crisis events which lead to physical, emotional and spiritual breakdown. It is my prayer and desire that more and more counselors, pastors and all other helpers would create the opportunity to educate people about crisis prevention and thus facilitate a greater number of people the opportunity to live more wholesome and functional lives.

My intention in this book is to help all people develop a lifestyle model that can effectively minimize or prevent crisis events and minimize dysfunctional responses to crisis events. Thereby equipping people to become more functionally whole in optimizing their service to God and fellow humans and maximizing God's purpose for their lives on this earth.

I have chosen to engage in this study because I consider it extremely urgent in this time of increasing instability and uncertainty over many things. Humanity has now entered the 3rd millennium and religious and secular prophets of doom and gloom will abound. Millions of people may experience even greater emotional and spiritual disequilibrium as this new millennium marches on. In fact, just before the close of the year 1999 millions were caught up in the Y2K mania spending much more money than normal in preparation for the collapse of society.

Since my pastoral ministry, which began in 1982, I have had occasion to counsel hundreds of Christians whose lives became destabilized by crises of every type. I have had to counsel people facing legal, financial, physical, marital, emotional, and spiritual crises. Within the last few years of my ministry in the city of New York I have seen more and more people whose lives have entered severe disequilibrium because of dysfunctional lifestyles of their parents or of themselves.

In most of these cases, these crises could have been prevented or considerably minimized if only they had had the proper education, the concerned guidance of others, their own

4

determined commitment to follow the path to minimize crisis and a deep personal relationship with Jesus Christ.

I, too, have had to battle against stress, depression and anger. I have often walked through the valley of despair to the point where I despaired of life and began to contemplate suicide as an attractive alternative to life. For years I struggled for survival and meaning in an abusive church whose pastor seemed to enjoy condemning and tormenting people rather than nurturing them with God's love. By God's grace, I was spared the dysfunctional responses but there were times I did consider engaging in behaviors that would have been self-destructive. God kept me secure in His love and eventually gave me the strength to get out of the spiritually abusive environment.

Far too many lives are wasted as millions of people live a lifestyle that paves the way for crisis after crisis, thus robbing them of their potential to make a difference for the kingdom of God. Too many lives are marginalized, not for lack of opportunity, but for lack of adequate knowledge and proper guidance. We need more people to live lives at the optimal level for serving God and making a positive difference for fellow humans.

It is my prayer and fervent hope that I can be used by God to help people avoid crises and the consequent suffering that normally accompany major crises and therefore become effective tools in the hands of God for nurturing others who truly need urgent help. It is my strong conviction that Christian counselors and pastors need to take a proactive approach to helping their clients and parishioners live more abundant lives, by teaching them how to develop and maintain a lifestyle that will minimize crisis and maximize functional wholeness and service for the Lord, Jesus Christ. It is critical that parents begin to implement the Christian lifestyle and teach their children the enduring value of such for the rest of their lives.

The pursuit of a lifestyle of wholeness and holiness in order to minimize crisis is really the core of preventive counseling. In the field of medical science most doctors are edu-

5

cated to treat illnesses and diseases. The tragedy is that millions of people could have avoided the need for medications or surgery had they been educated in preventive medicine. The idea is succinctly crystallized in a letter sent to Ann Landers in her well-known newspaper column. The writer chides Ann for not correctly handling a previous letter. She writes, *"I was surprised at your reply to 'Irritated with Doctors in Texas,' a 50 year old woman who had seen four doctors in five years, and not one of them had bothered to tell her that losing weight could reduce her blood pressure. You replied the problem was her poor selection of doctors.*

I think you missed the point. Most doctors have been trained to treat disease and disorders. They have very little education in nutrition and even less in preventive medicine. Drugs have been considered the first line of defense. Other forms of treatment are disregarded. The truth is, many medical problems can be prevented with proper diet, exercise and regular checkups. Fortunately, things are getting better. Medical schools are beginning to see the value in emphasizing training in nutrition and preventive medicine. We need doctors who not only can help us get well when we are sick but make sure we are healthy the rest of the time".[i]

I really was delighted to see Ann's response to this letter. *She replied, "You are absolutely right. In today's world, the key is making sure we are 'healthy the rest of the time'. The face of medical training has changed dramatically in the last 10 years. The focus is now on preventing illness rather than simply treating it. This trend should continue as HMOs discover that preventing disease costs a lot less than treating patients after illness sets in. Doctors are telling their patients to stop baking themselves in the sun to avoid skin cancer. Smoking is no longer chic. It is shunned because we know it causes lung cancer and other diseases. Exercise is touted for the heart. Mammograms are a must for women and prostate examinations are a must for men. All of the above add up to the wisdom of preventing problems before they occur. Makes sense, doesn't it?"[ii]*

The truth is that hundreds of millions of people can avoid medical crises if they learn preventive medicine. Therefore it is my position that it is equally important, indeed, even more important that Christian counselors and pastors and other helping professionals educate people in the method of preventing crises. Out of a desire to help people live more functionally whole lives and thus enjoy the abundant life that God intends I have been moved to write this book.

I am aware that some of the material I present in this study may make some people uncomfortable, causing great cognitive dissonance, because their very lifestyles are being challenged. But I am also aware that growth occurs in response to challenges. Often, we are conditioned by society in patterns of thinking that are self-destructive. We accept them, hardly ever questioning the efficacy of the lifestyle. We make the same mistakes of the preceding generation and we transmit the same dysfunctional lifestyle to another generation so that they too are doomed to repeat the same mistakes and be engulfed by the same crises. I submit that crisis prevention education, if diligently taught and applied and placed under the guidance of the Holy Spirit, can move us from the culture of crisis and death to the culture of wholeness and life.

1: The Nature and Dynamics of Crisis

The world is filled with crises. In fact, from the very beginning of human history life has been plagued with crises at international, national, community, family and personal levels. Every day, the news media bombard us with stories of crises as society continues to decay in very tragic ways with incalculable consequences for those who are responsible for the crises and for those who are simply the victims of the crises. Because of the frequency and intensity of crises it is my position that we need to equip counselors and clergy with information to help minimize the crisis events in this world and minimize the crisis responses, which are so common in a world, deceived by Satan.

It is of course necessary to define the word "crisis". Authors Swihart and Richardson explain crises in these terms, *"Essentially crisis events are changes in our world that necessitate emotional adjustment on our part. Usually they are produced by sudden and unexpected events; sometimes however, they are produced by anticipated happenings.*[iii] I propose that one cannot speak of crisis in a comprehensive way until one distinguishes between the crisis event and the crisis response.

A crisis event is any event that normally results in emotional disequilibrium within people. It must be understood that what may be a crisis event for one person may not be perceived as a crisis event for another. Hence the difficulty of securing complete accuracy and agreement in defining such terms. It is safer to speak of the crisis event in terms of conditions, which generally create disequilibrium in people.

Based on patterns of observable behavior it is quite reasonable to categorize some events as minor crisis events and others as major crisis events. Even in doing so a counselor needs to keep in mind that what may be a minor crisis event for one person may be generally perceived as a major crisis event for the majority.

Most counselors, psychologists and other mental health professionals will agree that some crisis events are far more stressful than others are. Thus it is generally maintained that the following events are considered within the category of the major crisis events. These include:

Death of spouse
Divorce
Marital separation
Imprisonment
Death of a family member
Personal injury or serious illness
Marriage
Loss of job
Marital reconciliation
Retirement

But even within this list it must be recognized that there are some people for whom the loss of gainful employment is a major crisis which can result in suicide while for some people the loss of a job may just be a minor setback and create no disequilibrium emotionally. The crisis response is not the same for all people even though they may experience the same event.

The difference in response is the result of a combination of several factors, some of which are: genetics, temperament, physical health, family dynamics, family history, cultural values, education, religious philosophy and the presence or absence of the Holy Spirit. The presence and utilization of the Holy Spirit is the most important factor in determining how a person will respond to the crisis circumstances in life.

Given the fact that our response system to crisis conditions is determined by several different factors working together. It is imperative that counselors and other helpers recognize and understand these differences. Failure to be sensitive to these differences may deepen and intensify the crisis of the victim. Every parent who has at least two children is well aware that he/she must be alert to the differences in the chil-

9

dren and will need to adopt different strategies with the children to achieve optimal results. It is tragic that we oftentimes paint all people with the same brush based on our own particular standards and expectations. Anybody who wishes to help the hurting must be sensitive to the differences in the nature and dynamics of crisis.

Minor stress events would create for some people a mild crisis. The emotional effects are not serious and the persons regain normalcy very soon. Such events may include a minor cold, a mild pain in the lower back, a late appointment, a canceled date, a phone call from a creditor, a failing grade in an exam and other such things. In these cases, for the most part, the victim does not lose equilibrium for any sustained length of time. It is a discomfort for a few hours or may be a day or two. Except in rare circumstances, the person does not really need counseling help. He or she is able to shake it off and pursue life. Of course, it should be realized that for a few persons who might be disordered in some way a call from a creditor might precipitate a major crisis. But since this is not the normative behavior it is permissible to consider such stressors as minor crisis events.

Another concern about crises is that it is not always possible to clearly demarcate between the crisis event and the response to the crisis. In fact, sometimes what is at one time a crisis event may be at another time or at the very same time a crisis response. Let me illustrate the complexity of this matter by use of a common example. It is common knowledge that alcohol abuse and alcoholism are very serious crises leading to numerous other crises as will be discussed later in this paper. The point is that we cannot clearly separate the event from the response. Consider, for example, that in many cases, the abuse of alcohol is a response to depression. The depression might have been the response to a marital crisis or a job termination. Notice the dynamics in the following case study.

The employee, Joe, is retrenched as a result of downsizing the company. The loss of this job is a lot more than a loss of a job. A chain reaction follows. The loss of the job implies a loss of financial support, which leads to a loss of social contacts, which leads to a loss of his emotional support systems. The weight of all these losses combined together causes Joe to become depressed. The depression is the dysfunctional response to the job loss.

In his emptiness and hopelessness, Joe seeks the friendship of alcohol to ease the pain of the losses. In the process, he finds a few new friends who are, for the most part, equally dysfunctional. But the use of the alcohol and the conversation with his new buddies neutralize a part of the pain of the original loss.

Soon, he becomes dependent on the alcohol to the point that he is unable to function effectively at home. In fact, his functional capacity is seriously impaired. His wife deserts him. The loss of his wife and family is more than he can handle. His depression darkens and deepens to the point of utter hopelessness. Feeling miserable, friendless, joyless and hopeless he goes to the ultimate step of a dysfunctional response to a crisis. He commits suicide after.

In this case study, we can understand that the crisis event and the crisis response are blurred; one feeds on the other or is generated by the other so that it is simultaneously the crisis event and the crisis response. This example is typical of numerous other crisis situations.

Hence my reason to develop a therapeutic model that deals with the whole person and the entire process. The well-intentioned mistake helpers may make is to think in mathematical terms. They deal with number one and then they move to number two.

Truly life would be very simple and easy if this numerical progression were the order and structure of life. Thus the skilled counselor must be cognizant of the fact of the complexity and imprecision of the nature and dynamics of crisis counseling whether as therapy for already existing crisis situations or as preventive counsel for potential crises.

In this book I will not be addressing the minor crisis events at all. My purpose is to deal with major crisis events and propose a lifestyle model, which can effectively minimize or prevent crisis events and minimize crisis responses thereby equipping people to become more functionally whole and, consequently, enhance their usefulness as instruments in God's service.

2: The Inevitability of Crisis

Having explained the nature and dynamics of crisis it is critical to understand that while I am proposing a lifestyle to minimize crisis and maximize one's life for God, I am not suggesting that life can be totally free from crisis. Crisis is a very part of the fabric of life. A person may make all the right choices nutritionally, physically, socially, financially, emotionally and spiritually and still have to deal with crisis situations in his/her life. (For the sake of simplicity I shall use the pronoun, him as representative of both sexes except in certain cases where it is grammatically required that I use the pronoun, her) The inevitable truth is that crisis cannot be totally avoided. Here is why no human can be completely free from crisis.

When God created mankind, He presented the first couple with a choice. The Holy Bible records this command, *"You are free to eat from any tree in the garden; but you must not eat from the tree of the knowledge of good and evil, for when you eat of it you will surely die."* (Gen. 2:16-17 / NIV). Thus God presented a choice. Adam and Eve chose to disobey and in the process ushered humanity into the worst crisis possible, the crisis of death. As a result of sin, the death sentence was imposed upon all humanity. It is theologically futile to debate what would have happened had the first humans not sinned. The fact is that they made a choice that makes crisis in human life inevitable.

God passed a sentence upon the human race as is recorded in Genesis 3:14-19. To Satan, He said, *"I will put enmity between you and the woman and between your offspring and hers; he will crush your head and you will strike his heel."* (Gen. 3:15 / NIV) Theologians generally agree that this enmity is referring to Satan's hatred of humans culminating in his persecution of Jesus Christ and subsequent crucifixion. Satan is the enemy of humanity and seeks to destroy what God has created.

Only God knows the number of crises generated by Satan. The unavoidable truth is that Satan is the enemy of God and will seek to create crisis in the lives of people to detract them from God's gift of eternal life and minimize their usefulness for the work of God. It is Satan's job to keep people in spiritual darkness. For those who have left his kingdom and entered the kingdom of God, it is Satan's job to attack them and minimize their effectiveness as instruments of God. As long as he is free to perform his tasks so long will humanity experience crisis conditions.

God also passed a sentence upon the woman. To the woman, He said, *"I will greatly increase your pains in childbearing; with pain you will give birth to children. Your desire will be to your husband and he will rule over you."* (Gen. 3:16 / NIV) So it is no surprise that women often experience much suffering and pain in childbirth and that the battle between the sexes still rages. This is an inevitable crisis event. It is natural law and cannot be removed except for divine intervention.

God placed a sentence upon the man also. To the man he said, *"Cursed is the ground because of you; through painful toil you will eat of it all the days of your life. It will produce thorns and thistles for you, and you will eat the plants of the field. By the sweat of your brow you will eat your food until you return to the ground, since from it you were taken; for dust you are and to dust you will return."* (Gen. 3:17-19 / NIV).

As a result, man has had to battle against the natural forces of planet earth to ensure his very survival. Like in the previous case, it is clear to see that crisis is a natural result of the sin of mankind. Mankind's survival will involve struggle and pain for all. Crisis is simply built into the very fabric of life.

In Romans 5:12, Paul, the Apostle, throws further light upon the inevitability of crisis when he writes, *"Therefore, just as sin entered the world through one man, and death through sin, and in this way death came to all men, because all sinned...."* (NIV). The point of all these Scriptures is to prove that crisis is inevitable. The physical body will decay and perish for it is mortal and therefore corruptible and perishable. So the crisis events of decay and death are not within our capacity to avoid.

To further illustrate the inevitability of crisis, let me direct attention to the natural disasters that occur frequently around the world. It is not uncommon for those of us living in the USA to experience hurricanes, tornadoes, snowstorms, earthquakes, floods and other similar disasters, which are beyond the control of even the best scientists on the planet. When such deadly disasters strike crises are generated. Such natural "acts of God" leave in its path all types of crises, financial, physical, medical, emotional and spiritual.

Often, thousands of people are rendered homeless or without basic essential services for their daily survival thus precipitating all types of crises. Of course, there is always the tragic crisis facing the surviving families and friends of those who would have lost their lives in these disasters. No amount of preventive counseling could prevent such crisis events from occurring as they often do in the USA and indeed, around the world.

Of course, natural disasters are not the exclusive "privilege" of Americans. Every nation on every continent experiences natural disasters. In November 1998 hurricane Mitch left over ten thousand people dead in Honduras and Nicaragua. This tragedy was beyond words. It precipitated a major crisis for hundreds of thousands of people. For such a crisis event there could not have been any preventive counseling. However, if the survivors had a right relationship with God then they could have avoided some of the dysfunctional responses that followed.

Yet another type of inevitable crisis is that which is the result of somebody else's mistake. In this scenario, the crisis could have been prevented if the blameworthy person had effectively done his job. But since the task was inadequately done a major crisis could potentially occur for unsuspecting victims. For example, if a pilot is flying an aircraft while under the influence of sufficient alcohol to impair his ability to maneuver the aircraft then it is likely that he will crash the plane. Hundreds of innocent people may end up with a major crisis in their lives if they survive, or their families may face the crisis if they die in the crash.

In the USA, every day, people suffer major accident injuries because the driver of another vehicle is under the influence of alcohol. In fact, thousands die every year as a result of driving while drunk. The crisis that ensues is for those left alive, as is often the case when teenagers get killed because of mixing alcohol with driving.

Of course, it should be obvious that drunkenness is preventable. The tragedy is when the drunken person crashes into the vehicle of the sober driver and kills him. The grieving family faces a crisis of major magnitude. The fact of life is that we cannot control the behavior of others. Unfortunately the wrong lifestyles of some often creates crises for others who may be pursuing the morally correct lifestyle.

Another type of inevitable crisis is where the victim is the offspring of a parent who did not take proper care of herself and consequently the child is born with a major defect. A sickly mother or one who fails to exercise her love for the unborn child by the ingestion of drugs and other dangerous substances, makes it highly probable that her child will suffer major health problems for a long time. This child endures a crisis because of the fault of the mother and cannot be held responsible for the crisis.

Tragically, millions of children are the victims of such situations and are doomed to lives of crisis conditions because of the sins of the parents. It is not uncommon for thousands of children to be born with AIDS because their parents were engaged in a sinful lifestyle. In fact, today in Africa millions of children are being severely affected by the crisis of AIDS. In such situations the child grows up with an ongoing physical and emotional crisis not through his own negligence but rather because of the failure of the parents. Tragically, as time goes on such children may enter into a spiritual crisis as they begin to blame God for their misfortune and thus find it very difficult to establish a right relationship with God.

I wish to describe one more type of crisis in which the victim is a victim of a situation beyond his control. The crisis is inevitable for the victim but could have been avoided if the one who caused it were willing to obey God's laws of love. I speak of the millions of people who historically and currently suffer religious and political oppression from the governing authorities which are constitutionally legitimate. It is certainly a crisis event to be tortured. Lamentably, even today thousands of Christians face this crisis daily only because of their loyalty to Jesus Christ in a society that despises Jesus.

According to the latest and most reliable sources Christians are facing arrest, imprisonment, physical torture and even death in several countries. Such countries include Afghanistan, Algeria, Azerbaijan, Bangladesh, Bhutan, Brunei, China, Comoro Islands, Cuba, Cyprus, Egypt, Indonesia, Iran, Iraq, Kuwait, Laos, Malaysia, Mauritania, Morocco, Burma, Nigerian, North Korea, Oman, Pakistan, Qatar, Saudi Arabia, Somalia, Sri Lanka, Sudan, Syria, Tajikistan, Tunisia, Turkey, Vietnam and Yemen. I list these countries to illustrate the magnitude of the tragedy facing Christians who suffer such crises not because of their own doing but because of the fallen condition of mankind.

The foregoing information is not by any means exhaustive nor was it intended to be. It is to highlight the fact that crisis in life is not totally avoidable. In the next two sections I will present the model for minimizing crisis living. But one must not be naïve to believe that it is possible to live a lifestyle, which eliminates all crises. Humans can prevent or minimize many crisis events in their lives but we cannot be under the illusion that by doing all the right things we may prevent all crises. The reality is that mankind lives in a fallen world, a world of sin, decay and death; a world in which Satan seeks to bring misery upon people to rob them of the joy which God intends.

The proper understanding of the theology of crisis can serve to actually lessen the pain of the crisis event and minimize the dysfunctional response to the crisis. This includes a spiritual awareness of the fall of mankind, the effects of sin, the role of Satan as the enemy of God and all humanity, the grace of God, and the role of the Holy Spirit. Thus counselors must be able to help their counselees, parents help their children, teachers help their students, pastors help their parishioners understand this essential theology of crisis as a fact of life and not perceive their crises always as the results of their own failures and sinfulness. In fact, to place blame on people for crises that were outside of their control is to weigh them down with the heavy burden of guilt that would cause an even greater crisis leading to severe emotional dysfunction.

3: Preventing or Minimizing the Crisis Event

To acknowledge that some crises are inevitable does not leave the human totally at the mercy of his environment. God designed us to make decisions and very often the decisions we make will determine the type of life we live. The fact of the matter is that for millions of people who experience crisis in their lives they could have avoided or at least minimized the crises and the resulting disequilibrium. Wrong decisions will naturally tend to bring dysfunctional results. Tragically, in many cases people make unwise decisions for lack of knowledge. Even worse are the numerous cases where people make unwise decisions fully cognizant of the destructive pattern of behavior but lack the self-control and discipline to change their course of thinking and acting.

Let me illustrate a crisis, which could have been avoided, had the person exercised wisdom in making the sensible choices. Joanna is only 17years old. She has a story to tell, a story that can serve to help other teenagers and even adults to think through their decisions carefully before engaging in behavior which would later produce a crisis. *"I am 17 and I like to laugh, play, study, party and be carefree. There is one part of my life, however, that makes me different from other girls my age. I became a mother at age 16. I made a bad decision to have sex too young, without thinking about the consequences. Tonight, I am missing the party of the year, because I cannot afford a babysitter, not to mention a new dress. I am also a year behind in school and on home studies. My baby boy is almost 2 and I have not seen his father since I told him I was pregnant. I own two pairs of pants, three shirts and shoes off the bargain table at the discount store, because the baby's needs are expensive and constant. For those who think having a baby will turn you into a free adult, it won't. Here is what you get to do:*

19

Wake up for 2a.m. feeding. For months, I did not have more than five hours of sleep a night.

Wake out of a sound sleep to care for a sick or frightened baby when you can't even think straight yourself.

Lug a diaper bag, baby stroller and irritable baby everywhere.

Never have a penny to spend on cute new clothes or makeup.

Lose your friends and disappoint your family.

I am begging all teenagers to think twice before having sex. See the world first. Go to college. Above all, enjoy your teen years. The opposite sex will always be there, but you can be a teenager only once."[iv]

Joanna's story is not an isolated case. She is just one among millions of teenagers who by reason of a sinful choice, are embarking on a road that will lead to major crisis events and severe disequilibrium emotionally, financially, socially, and spiritually. It is essential that parents and schoolteachers and other adults teach the youths in their charge the wisdom of right moral choices. We must never forget that Joanna's crisis in not just her crisis. It becomes a crisis for the rest of her family, her school friends and ultimately, for her child who, perhaps, will never enjoy the blessings of a family the way God intended.

There can be no doubt as one listens to Joanna and the millions like her in this world that this crisis could have been prevented. She admitted it was a "bad decision". The fact of the matter is that every day millions of people are making decisions that, for the moment, seem beneficial and enjoyable but, later on, will precipitate a major crisis event and response that would negatively affect the rest of their lives. In Proverbs 16:25 we are told that, *"There is a way that seems right to a man but in the end it leads to death."*

I wish to use another example, this time, concerning an adult to show how unwise decisions can lead to major crises. As in the previous case this crisis was totally avoidable if the person had exercised self-control. In the industrialized world the computer has become a major tool of communication and dissemination of information. I thank God for the computer. Without it the writing of this book would be a very slow and tedious process. Further, I was able to surf the web, go on line and search out information relevant to my research for this book.

This access to an incredible wealth of information is fascinating and very useful if used properly. But the lamentable truth is that, like many other things which sinful mankind has misused, the Internet is being used as a tool of Satan to destroy thousands of lives. I suppose no one really knows the numbers of people whose lives have been and are being negatively impacted by the Internet. On the Internet are available thousands of sites that facilitate the sexual lust of insecure and unfulfilled people. In a recent article appearing in the *Daily News* an estimate of porno addicts was given. I quote, *"At least 20,000 Internet users are 'cybersex compulsives' hooked on porn sites, X-rated chat rooms or other sexual materials online"*. [v]

Surely, this is a very conservative estimate. I suspect that the real figures are much higher given the fact the porn sites are increasing almost daily. The fact that such sites are on the increase indicates that it is a lucrative business. Obviously the number of cybersex clients is rapidly increasing.

The consequences are frightening as thousands of humans of all ages enter a roadway in cyberspace that will lead them to major crises in their marriages and families. The research has found that compulsives have far more problems with relationships and jobs than those who are not porn addicts do. This obsession with Internet pornography, X-rated chat rooms and online sex affairs is wreaking havoc in millions of lives. Here is one example. We will call her, Dorothy. Let her tell her story:

"Dear Ann: I had to write when I read the letter from 'At Wits' End in the Midwest,' whose husband was addicted to the Internet. I realized that I, too, was addicted. I did everything possible to be on line at a certain hour for a chat with

the man of my dreams. I missed several appointments, left meetings early and decided against taking a night class because I might not be home in time to chat with this fabulous man whom I had never met. In retrospect, I now know I was totally hooked on this person. I am not a brainless ditz. I am a churchgoing woman, the mother of four children and active in the PTA. No one would believe I was behaving like a lovestruck teenager.

We are no longer chatting. After five months, he dropped me and moved on. I was devastated. I am still not completely over him. Thank God, my husband is a wonderful and patient man. He has stayed by my side through this whole ordeal. I am in counseling and trying to get my head together. My advice to any Internet chatter is to realize you are at risk. I wasted a lot of valuable hours on what started out as a pastime and ended up being an obsession. The night my Internet lover told me it was all over between us because his wife felt threatened, I cried myself to sleep. Please warn your readers, Ann. Tell them how dangerous and destructive the Internet can be.[vi]

This story is powerful in several ways and certainly helps me make my case for preventive counseling and the lifestyle of holiness in order to avoid crisis. When we consider that Dorothy was a "churchgoing woman" we can understand the power of Satan to cause people, even those who profess to have changed spiritually, to lose focus, engage in unhealthy behavior oblivious to the danger signs along the road because their unhealthy obsession blinds them to the destination. Soon enough the ride along this road will hit a huge pothole and devastation will occur. The truth is that Dorothy was traveling along the road to a crisis. At some point along the road the crisis event would occur because the necessary environmental conditions and an unholy spiritual climate were being forged. All too often the person who is engaged in this journey cannot see the destruction ahead because she is too focused on earthly things.

The Wholeness & Holiness Model

I wish to propose a very simple (simple in terms of a statement, but not in accomplishment) lifestyle model. Properly understood, developed and implemented, this model will significantly minimize or prevent crisis events. The exception for these are inevitable by reason of the natural creative process, the sin of others, or the divine will of the Sovereign God, to permit a crisis in our lives for His glory and our spiritual growth. The following analogy will serve to underscore the lifestyle model I am proposing.

Consider the case of Flash who goes to the auto dealer and purchases a flashy, exquisite, state of the art automobile. He is given an instruction booklet that meticulously explains the procedures for maintenance to ensure the optimum functioning of this vehicle. Flash drives home with excitement and a sense of great pride. Thinking of the respect he would now receive from the people in his community as he sports his flashy, new auto, he drives around the neighborhood, makes long drives, tours the countryside, and simply enjoys the freedom and prestige of this marvelous piece of modern technology. Of course, he refuels whenever it is required and often spends time washing and polishing the vehicle. He thinks that he is maintaining his vehicle based on what he sees.

According to the instruction manual the vehicle requires an oil change and fluid check every three thousand miles. Several other maintenance checks are required. But Flash is too busy enjoying the popular life with his friends and family to make the time for the necessary preventive maintenance checks. Some of his friends remind him of the need to take his car back to the dealer to do a full service check and Flash acknowledges the need to do so.

But the vehicle is working well. The exterior is still exquisite and he has not experienced any engine troubles; no danger signals have been manifested. And so he reasons that all is well. Six months have elapsed without an oil and filter change. The lubricating effectiveness of the oil is gone; hard deposits are beginning to form inside the engine and diminish the overall effectiveness of the vehicle but Flash is so much in love with the pleasure of driving that the little signals do not even get his attention. What Flash does not know is that his vehicle is about to experience a major breakdown. All the lubricants have lost their efficiency and the water coolant is almost finished.

One glorious summer day Flash is on his way to Toronto from New York. Together with his few friends they are hoping for a great vacation in Toronto. After eight hours of driving the night has fallen and as Flash is attempting to overtake another vehicle, suddenly his engine breaks down and the car lurches to the side of the road into a ditch. He and his friends panic as they realize that they are a long way from home and are in a very deserted area of the country. Panic! Fear! Desperation! Confusion!

Flash is devastated. I do not need to go any further. By failing to act in accordance with the manual Flash set himself up for this crisis event. Had he diligently followed the maintenance schedule Flash would have at least reduced the number of crises in his life by one.

Lamentably, many people treat their body, soul and spirit the same way Flash treated his fancy car. For the most part, people tend to live life based on outward appearance. They do not think in terms of preventive measures. The goals of money, power and sexual satisfaction are so dominant that the more critical aspects of life are not regularly checked and serviced. For millions of people, the focus is too much on the superficial outside and not on the critical inside where major decay and corrosion are taking place without their awareness

And then, one day, suddenly, they crash as their engines come to a halt. They are towed to a hospital, in an ambulance, for a massive overhaul. What a tragedy that the large majority of people live their lives without real purpose, structure, growth strategy, maintenance schedule and preventive care. It is my firm conviction that if people would be willing to follow the instruction manual on right living, they would develop a lifestyle that would significantly reduce the crisis pattern of living, minimize their need for crisis counseling and maximize their lives for The Holy God.

The lifestyle model I submit is based on two key words: **wholeness and holiness**. Before I delve into the dynamics and methodology of both I should make a few important observations about these two words. Wholeness and holiness are not necessarily the same thing. When I speak of wholeness I am using this terminology to mean the balanced integration of the physical, mental, emotional and spiritual dimensions of life to enable one to be functionally stable and in control of one's life. This is not an easy accomplishment for it involves a calculated disciplinary effort to develop one's capacity to its fullest in these diverse but interdependent areas of one's life.

Holiness refers to the unique relationship that a human can have with God through the redemptive and mediative work of Jesus Christ. A Christian can be physically dysfunctional by reason of a disease and yet attain to holiness. So, holiness is possible without wholeness. Holiness implies the pursuit of developing the mind and character of Jesus Christ. It involves Christ being formed within the Christian. And yet, such a person may experience a major crisis by neglecting the laws that govern health. In reality, holiness is only possible to the extent that a person allows Jesus Christ to live in him by the sanctifying work of the Holy Spirit. The pursuit of holiness is, therefore, the process of sanctification is the response to God's grace in His justification of us.

The above distinction is particularly important when a Christian counselor may have to work with a non-Christian. It is possible to explain the principles of wholeness by which the person may avoid major crises and the dysfunctional responses to such crises and not coerce the person to accept Jesus Christ.

Of course, in one sense, it can be correctly argued that a person who does not know Jesus cannot be whole. But since counselors deal with people who are non-Christian and we know that several non-Christians can live lives that are functionally stable and wholesome I consider it wise to make the

25

distinction between wholeness and holiness. Hence the reason for the term "holiness". For the Christian, holiness is not optional; it is a command. And most assuredly the pursuit of holiness would serve particularly well in the minimization of dysfunctional responses to crisis events. I will address this subject in the next chapter.

It is critical to all that seek to become whole and holy understand that we cannot establish very defined lines of demarcation among the three dimensions of wholeness. So even though, for the sake of structure in presenting the information I will address each dimension separately, we need to be fully cognizant of the connectedness of all three. The fact is that the physical impacts the emotional, which impacts the spiritual.

It is also true to state that the spiritual impacts the emotional, which impacts the physical. And it is equally true to claim that the emotional impacts the spiritual, which impacts the physical. The essential fact is humans need to understand the intricate design of being human so that we can move in the direction of wholeness and not attempt to separate that which cannot be separated.

Within the last few years much has been written about the subject of wholeness. In many of the books and articles that deal with this subject the writers reflect the value system and culture of the New Age Movement. I wish to categorically state in this book that I do not subscribe to New Age philosophy. It is man's effort to heal himself without the need for Jesus Christ. The term "wholeness" is not the property of those who subscribe to New Age philosophy. Christians have a right to use the word within the biblical parameters.

In fact, Christians have more to offer in this matter of wholeness because wholeness, in the most complete sense of the word, is not possible without Jesus Christ. The New Age movement is a counterfeit to real Christianity. It is often dressed up in very appealing and attractive garbs.

For this reason many, even within the Christian world, have succumbed to this deception which is worldwide and growing at an alarming rate. It uses language and terminology that are spiritual, even biblical, at times, but it is a mask for something, which is diabolical.

In their book, The *Seduction of Christianity,* authors Hunt and McMahon warn Christians that the New Age movement *"involve things that are firmly entrenched within the church, such as psychotherapy, visualization, meditation, biofeedback, positive confession, possibility thinking, hypnosis, Holistic medicine, and a whole spectrum of self-improvement and success/motivation techniques".* [vii]

The fact that several Christian churches have already begun to use these terms and apply them reflects the subtlety, power and pervasiveness of New Age thinking. But Christian counselors and Christians must insist on being Christian and recognize the inherent danger in the utilization of such methods. In essence the New Age philosophy rejects the deity of Jesus Christ and, in fact, proclaims Him as one of the trailblazers of the New Age. One Christian author who has researched the subject of New Age warns Christians that New Agers claim that *"Jesus is not the unique, unrepeatable and unsurpassable incarnation of a personal God, but rather a manifestation of a universal state of consciousness that anyone can attain through proper techniques".* [viii] In the light of such information, I wish to dissociate my concepts of "wholeness and holiness" from any New Age philosophy. I believe that the concept of wholeness is indeed a very biblical and fundamental principle in the prevention and minimization of crisis.

The Holy God of the Bible reveals Himself as the Creator of all things, including, human beings. He created the body, soul and spirit. In **Genesis 2:7** we read: *"The Lord God formed man from the dust of the ground (the physical body) and breathed into his nostrils the breath of life (Hebrew word neshamah, meaning the human spirit), and man became a living being (Hebrew word nephesh, which can mean "soul")."*
In **I Thessalonians 5:23** Paul writes: *...May your whole spirit, soul and body be kept blameless at the coming of our Lord, Jesus Christ."* These scriptures illustrate the reality of the three dimensional human. Several Christian authors, writing

on the subject of wholeness, have maintained that *"human beings are made up of three distinct but interrelated parts."*[ix] The fact is that God has created humans with these three dimensions and these three were meant to work as an integrated whole. Failure to develop any one dimension can and often does adversely affect the other parts. In the same way, the development of any one part can and often does positively impact upon the other parts.

Drs. Richard and Phyllis Arno integrate these three in these words, *"You are a spiritual being, you possess a soul and you live in a body. Everyone knows it is possible to develop or educate your mind (your mind is part of your soul), and everyone also knows you can develop your body by exercise. Since it is true that you can develop your mind and your body, it must also be possible to develop your spirit. God would not give man the capacity for developing the mind and body without including man's spirit-or else man would not have been created a spiritual being."*[x]

The purpose of quoting a few authors on this matter is simply to make my point that the human ought to be cared for from the perspective of wholeness, the integration of the three major parts of the human; and not as isolated parts. (It is not my intention in this book to engage in a theological/philosophical discussion on defining the lines of demarcation among the three parts. Rather, it is my purpose to make a case for counselors to help people prevent or minimize crises in life by dealing with all three parts of the human being. Therefore, any overlap between the body, soul/mind and spirit is deliberate in my effort to present wholeness and holiness as a lifestyle model for the prevention and minimization of crisis.

4. Physical Wholeness

Millions of Americans, and indeed, humans all over the world, are on the road to a major crisis because they neglect the critical aspects of the physical dimension of their beings. Too often, in the rush to make money or enjoy the pleasures of the flesh or because of plain laziness people do not really make a concerted effort to develop their health. And so the grim statistics remind us every day of the results of wrong health habits. Eating nutritionally dead foods (junk foods), sitting in front of television sets (and becoming "couch potatoes"), imbibing alcohol in dangerous amounts, filling their lungs with deadly cigarette smoke, spending too much time carousing, all of which robs them of adequate sleep and rest.

The fact of the matter is that it seems that the majority of Americans are not concerned about honoring God in their bodies. The tragedy is that millions of people at this very moment are living a lifestyle guaranteed to bring them to a major health crisis that, in turn, would create a major emotional and spiritual crisis.

I submit that most people do not like to deal with this subject because it elicits feelings of guilt over their own wrong health habits. This, in itself, is another problem that manifests a lack of wholeness. The emotional baggage that some people carry is often the reason they are unable to shake themselves from the inactivity. They rationalize, justify and even legitimize their lack of commitment to a healthy lifestyle. So in one sense, some people need to deal with their emotional inadequacies before they can even get off their laurels and begin a program of adopting fitness and physical health as essential priorities.

The fundamental truth is simply that if people want to minimize physical health crises they must seek to achieve wholeness in the physical dimension of their lives. Failure to do so is an act of self-destruction, not intentionally, of course, but by neglect to use proven principles to maintain healthy bodies. Additionally, Christians should consider that God requires us to honor Him in our bodies.

Diet

Today there are thousands of books on physical health. One common theme among them is the need to know and understand and practice the natural laws of health to avoid the major diseases that are common crises. According to Dr. Jethro Kloss, *"Many who violate the laws of health are ignorant of the relations between the laws of living (eating, drinking and working) to their health. Until they have some kind of sickness or illness, they do not realize their condition is caused by violating the laws of nature and health. If then they would resort to simple means, and follow the simple laws of health that they have been neglecting – proper diet, use of pure water, fresh air, sunshine, rest, and natures remedies, herbs, etc., nature would restore the body to its original health."*[xi]

Consider for example the crisis of cancer in the world, especially in the U.S. According to Newsweek dated November 30th 1998, it was estimated that by the end of 1998 about 95,600 would be victims of colon/rectal cancer, 184,500 with prostate cancer, 180,300 with breast cancer and 171,500 with lung cancer. In this very article the writers make the claim that proper diet and a healthy lifestyle can reduce colon/rectal cancer by about 75%, prostate cancer by 20%, breast cancer by about 50% and lung cancer by about 95%. To quote directly, *"Researchers estimate that diets filled with fruits and vegetables instead of fats – along with exercise and weight control – could eventually reduce cancer incidence by 30 to 40 percent. That would amount to 3 million to 4 million fewer cases per year worldwide. Diet and lifestyle may be particularly effective in preventing America's four leading malignancies: prostate, breast, colon and lung cancer".*[xii]

There is mounting evidence to verify that cancer and several other diseases are the result of an unhealthy lifestyle. I quote from yet another publication to prove that diet and exercise are critical factors in cancer and therefore, if people are willing to pursue wholeness in health there would be less cancer and fewer crises in this tottering world. *"Cancer may be less of a mystery than it appears. Worldwide, it strikes ten million people a year. Experts estimate that 30 to 40 percent of those cancers could be prevented by healthier diets and exercise. Eating fruits and vegetables alone could eliminate 20 percent. Last year, the World Cancer Research Fund and the American Institute for Cancer Research issued a comprehensive report on how we could slash cancer rates simply by changing what we eat and how much we exercise. John D. Potter of the Fred Hutchinson Cancer Research Center in Seattle chaired the panel that wrote the report that reviewed more than 4,500 studies to reach its conclusions. Potter's message: While there are no guarantees, there is plenty you can do to cut your risk."*[xiii]

In an interview with Dr. Potter, the question was asked: Which diets cut cancer risk? Here is his answer: *"It has become absolutely clear that a diet high in vegetables and or fruit – that is, a diet high in plant foods- is associated with a lower risk of cancers at almost all sites".*[xiv]

What is the clear message from all this research? I think it is obvious! Human beings can have a significant degree of control in the minimization of health crises. The real problem, perhaps, is that millions of people have become habituated to eating foods that are nutritionally detrimental to physical health. People have become victims of destructive lifestyles and want the easy way to health.

For millions of Americans, they would prefer to continue indulging themselves in unhealthful diets and find some pill, drug, or medication to offset the ill effects of unwise dietary choices. With such a mindset it is no surprise that some who have contracted lung cancer have actually proceeded to sue the tobacco companies for damages to their health. It is this kind of irresponsibility that creates much suffering in this world today.

The fact of the matter is if people became more educated about health and were willing to discipline themselves to and take personal responsibility most health crises would be eliminated. But unfortunately and tragically many still persist in wrong dietary habits and so must pay the price as they move from one health crisis to another.

I consider it appropriate to mention here that it is this folly in our personal health care system that is one reason for the exorbitant cost of health care in this nation. For that reason many cannot afford health insurance which itself is another crisis. Perhaps, it is time for the leaders in government and medicine to tell the people the real truth about health and legislate accordingly. Of course, even health legislation will not change the dysfunctional habits of people.

It is instructive for us to heed the warnings of medical experts. *"In the three decades since Richard Nixon hauled off and declared war on cancer, America has spent billions pursuing better ways to kill malignant tumors. The quest has generated valuable knowledge and many new therapies. Yet our cancer death rate is roughly the same today as it was in 1970. Despite the best efforts of surgeons and oncologists, Americans die of breast, colon and prostate cancer at five to thirty times the rate of people in many parts of the world. In Thailand and Sri Lanka, somewhere between two and five of every 100,000 women die of breast tumors. In the United States, 30 to 490 meet that fate."*[xv]

One may well ask why such a discrepancy in the cancer death rates between the US and the other countries listed. An obvious answer is the dietary habits of the nations. Here in America, we stuff ourselves with over processed foods, lots of fatty foods, chemically poisoned foods and foodless foods. In most third world nations cancer is not as big a crisis as in the US because the diet is more natural and less refined.

So diet is a critical factor in health. The same article goes on to say, *"No one denies that diet is a large part of the reason. In a comprehensive analysis published last year, scientists assembled by the World Cancer Research Fund and the*

American Institute for Cancer Research concluded that poor eating habits account for a third of all cancer – roughly the same proportion attributable to smoking.[xvi]

The tragic fact is that millions of people, including the youth who will become the leaders of tomorrow, are living a lifestyle that is guaranteed to make them dysfunctional and spend their lives in regrets and hopelessness. Consider for example, the increasing use of drugs. According to a recent article that appeared in Newsday, the trends are alarming. *"Heroin use has risen rapidly among U.S. teens, with many middle-class youngsters snorting the drug in the mistaken belief that it's less addictive than shooting up, experts say. The proportion of America's 12th graders who use heroin doubled between 1990 and 1996, from 0.9 percent to 1.8 percent, according to a study yesterday in the journal Pediatrics. And the rate edged up again in 1997, to 2.1 percent, said the study's author, Dr. Richard H. Schwartz of the Iowa Hospital for Children in Iowa Falls Church, Va.*

Dr. Alan I. Leshner, director of the National Institute on Drug Abuse, said, "There's been an increase in purity of heroin on the street, and that increase in purity is drawing a generation of heroin sniffers, snorters and intranasal users, rather than injectors. They foolishly think if you don't inject it, it's not addicting, which is incredibly wrong. And so you're seeing middle class, upper middle-class yuppies using heroin, where five years ago they wouldn't go near it."[xvii]

Before I leave the subject of diet there is one more critical concern I should mention. I do this knowing that many people would take offense with this information by reason of their own addiction to the product. Nutritional research increasingly is establishing the connection between a sugar-laden diet and diverse diseases.

The sorry picture is that most Americans are addicted to refined sugar. And it is a dangerous obsession. Many Christian counselors will be afraid to address this matter because they themselves are afflicted with the sugar addiction. If we wish to be Christians of integrity then we must face the facts even when the information makes us uncomfortable.

33

Sugar addiction is responsible for millions of people experiencing major health crises. If we really want to prevent health crises or minimize them then the subject of sugar needs to be boldly faced and intelligently expedited. It is critical that we get out of the comfort Zone. This comfort zone in the matter of sugar leads to major discomfort years later.

Today, many health and wellness experts refer to sugar as "white death". And this is not an alarmist sentiment. It is based on solid scientific research and observable evidence in the lives of millions of people. William Duffy was once a sugar addict until he came under the influence of a woman who changed his life. Subsequently, he wrote a book, Sugar Blues, exposing the historical obsession with sugar and revealing the frightening consequences of a diet loaded with sugar. He writes, *"Refined sugar is lethal when ingested by humans because it provides only that which nutritionists describe as empty or naked calories. In addition, sugar is worse than nothing because it drains and leeches the body of precious vitamins and minerals through the demand its digestion, detoxification and elimination make upon one's entire system.*

Sugar taken every day produces a continuously overacid condition, and more and more minerals are required from deep in the body in the attempt to rectify the imbalance. Finally, in order to protect the blood, so much calcium is taken from the bones and teeth that decay and general weakening begin. Excess sugar eventually affects every organ in the body."[xviii] Most people are totally oblivious of such information because the major industries that push the consumption of sugar would prefer to keep people uninformed in order that they may continue to make profits while millions perish.

The tragedy unfolding every day is that millions of children and adults are stuffing themselves with sugar-laden foods in an effort to get quick energy totally unaware that they are traveling a road to major crises in their physical and emotional health. The current scientific research proves that too much sugar can lead to a poor immune system, diabetes, obesity, tooth and gum disease, migraine and heart disease. So what should people do?

Common sense would dictate that we must make every effort to significantly reduce the intake of refined sugar. This would involve a massive revolution in dietary patterns and put an end to the soda and confectionery industries. Every choice carries a result and so counselors need to educate people to make an informed choice.

The subject of diet is a very big one. I do not feel the need to say anymore on this subject. Thousands of excellent books are now available on proper nutrition. You the reader must decide whether you want to continue to be a slave to wrong habits and face the deadly consequences or challenge yourself to make the necessary corrections and reap the life-long benefits. Would you prefer to spend the final years of your life confined to pills, hospital visits, medications, invasive surgery and other such "exciting" things or leisurely enjoying a cruise on the seas of the Caribbean?

Exercise

Yet another way to achieve physical wholeness and minimize health-related crises is the discipline of physical exercise. Across America, today, millions are recognizing the tremendous value of exercising to maintain fitness and lessen the risk of certain types of diseases. But yet, many counselors and pastors do not transmit this vital information to their clients nor do they practice any forms of exercise. Too many adults prefer to spend their free hours in the sedentary position, viewing trash on television or drinking and eating junk. Incidentally the time spent on television often proves emotionally and spiritually damaging to most people.

The evidence for the health benefits of regular exercise is overwhelming as study after study demonstrates this fact which is now being accepted by the scientific community. Newsday ran an article eulogizing the benefits of exercise in the hope of encouraging people to get off their sedentary lifestyles and engage in a healthy lifestyle.

Dr. Steven Blair, an epidemiologist of the Cooper Institute for Aerobics Research in Dallas comments that, *"because of all the labor-saving devices that have become standard since World War II, we've just about engineered human energy expenditure out of existence. I don't think many of us are going to volunteer to go back and live in the Stone Age, but I do think we need to build some of this energy expenditure back into our lives, by increasing the amount of routine activity."* [xix] In this same article, Newsday commented that *"the importance of this was driven home in July 1996 when the Surgeon General's office – echoing similar recommendations made by the Centers for Disease Control and Prevention, the National Institutes of Health and virtually every other major public health organization in the country – made its pronouncement on the relationship of exercise to improved health, urging Americans to accumulate 30 minutes of moderate physical activity, most days of the week."* Why would such a recommendation be made? Because exercise can save life and facilitate the enjoyment of life by minimizing health crises. It is imperative that people educate themselves about health and become disciplined in the pursuit of a healthy lifestyle so as to minimize health problems.

According to the same article the Cooper Institute did a long-term study on very large populations. They tracked the health and lifestyle habits of 30,000 individuals over nearly 30 years. What were the results? The results *"show that people who are active – again, not necessarily running marathons, but just walking, gardening, moving – are far less likely to die prematurely, far less likely to suffer from high blood pressure, certain forms of cancer, adult diabetes and many other physiological and psychological problems. In fact, the research suggests that regular sessions of moderate activity can reduce premature mortality rates by as much as 50 percent.*[xx]

This should be exciting news for the estimated 50 million Americans who live a completely sedentary lifestyle. Such people have a choice to make. They may choose to remain in a sedentary lifestyle and run the risk of major health crises or develop a regular exercise routine and minimize the health crises and thus enjoy a more functionally wholesome life

According to the health specialists and fitness experts exercise can have several positive benefits on the human body. Here are some of the more commonly known benefits of consistent exercise:

The heart actually becomes larger. The workload given to the heart each time aerobic exercise is performed forces the heart muscle to actually grow larger and stronger.

The stroke volume of the heart increases. Each beat of a larger, more fit heart delivers greater amount of nutrient-rich blood to hard working muscles. Thus the heart will beat slower and with greater pumping performance while using energy more efficiently.

The body uses oxygen more efficiently by developing its aerobic metabolism capability. The lungs increase in size and breathing capacity also increases.

The body increases its number of capillaries. To meet the demand from more active muscles, the circulatory system build new capillaries to deliver greater blood flow to the working muscular areas. Since blood brings oxygen and carries away waste products, the body begins to enhance its cleansing action.

The ratio of fat to muscle changes. Aerobic exercise burns fat for energy and thus decreases the stores of fat in the body on condition that the person has a low fat diet. Simultaneously, lean muscle mass increases to meet the workload of regular exercise.

The body burns calories more efficiently. Thus at a high level of physical fitness, a person may consume more calories and not gain weight.

Exercise helps with psychological and emotional coping. By conditioning the body to become more efficient and produce larger amounts of energy, exercise gives one the ability to cope with stress and other emotional issues much better. When we consider that millions of people suffer heart attacks we are talking about millions of people experiencing crises which could have been prevented had they implemented the right fitness programs in pursuit of physical wholeness. The truth is that unlike a century ago when we did not have a scientific understanding of disease we now have significant knowledge that can be applied to prevent disease. While it is true that genetics plays a role in our predisposition to certain diseases over which we have limited control, it is also true that *"more important are self-destructive behavior patterns and lifestyle habits such as lack of exercise, smoking, inadequate diet and abuse of alcohol and drugs."xxi*

To summarize this section on physical wholeness I quote from a study course on fitness put out by the ICS School of Fitness and Nutrition. They make reference to a study done by the University of California, Los Angeles, of health behavior for over five and one-half years from 7,000 adult males. The results *"showed that increased life expectancy and better health related significantly to certain basic behaviors. These included:*

> *Eating three meals a day at regular times,*
> *instead of irregular snacks.*
> *Making an important daily meal of breakfast.*
> *Engaging in moderate exercise several times a week.*
> *Getting seven or eight hours of sleep each night.*
> *Avoiding smoking.*
> *Keeping weight at moderate levels.*
> *Using alcohol only in moderation, if at all.xxii*

The reality of the human body is that it must be cared for in a way that promotes well being. Like the automobile that requires the right type of fuel, oil, lubricants and general care so too with the human body. Drivers, like Flash, who only adorn the exterior of their vehicles soon, suffer a breakdown of their vehicles that may cost thousands of dollars to repair if it is at all reparable. Humans who decorate the exterior of their bodies with fancy clothes, perfumes and expensive jewelry while neglecting to feed the body with the right foods and discipline the body with the necessary aerobic and anaerobic exercises will suffer a major health crisis. This could cost thousands of dollars or, worse, die a premature death and leave others with an emotional crisis. The very God who designed the body also set in motion laws that govern health but the majority of people are too obsessed with the pursuit of money, status, power, sexual delights and other carnal pleasures so they fail to glorify God in their bodies. Life is about choices. Those who make the wrong choices about diet and exercise cannot expect to avoid the automatic consequences of such wrong choices. If we sow destruction to the flesh then we shall reap destruction. It is my view that Christian counselors and clergymen must address such matters as a basic education to all whom they counsel if they really want to provide substantial help to humanity.

5. Mental/Emotional Wholeness

I have given considerable attention to the physical dimension of wholeness as a lifestyle model that can effectively minimize, and in numerous cases, prevent major crises. I wish now to address the emotional aspect of wholeness. Let me reiterate the necessity of understanding the interconnectedness of all three, physical, mental/emotional and spiritual. The wholeness approach cannot be compartmentalized as clearly distinct and separate from each other. The scientific research makes it unquestionably clear that all three are interdependent and must therefore be treated as an integrated unit. I should also clarify that in this section there will be frequent overlap between the emotional and the spiritual, but the focus will be the emotional.

The most obvious question is: "What are emotions?" The most obvious answer is that emotions are feelings. This response is, perhaps, the best since most people understand emotions in terms of feelings. Social psychologist, Dr. Mary Vander Goot commenting on the difficulty of defining emotions says, *"...emotions or feelings are complex, mercurial, and evasive when we try to catch them with definitions".xxiii* I think that when we hear words like, anger, fear, happiness, guilt, excitement we know we are speaking of emotions.

Before I proceed any further, I need to establish a very critical point concerning emotions and wholeness. An emotion does not and cannot just exist by itself. In other words, an emotion is not independently self-existing. It is dependent upon something else. This something else is the mind. The wholeness approach to the human involves the balanced integration of the body, mind and spirit. The emotions belong to the mind. In fact, the mind has three functions: intellect, emotions and will. So to speak of emotional wholeness requires mental soundness. And mental soundness is often dependent upon the spiritual component.

How can one therefore define emotional wholeness? This may be an easy question to ask but there is no easy answer. In some cultures the anger response to any frustration may be considered the right response but medically and spiritually it is detrimental to the person. Therefore, I will use the Christian parameters. Emotional wholeness is the ability and capacity to experience and manifest, where appropriate, the wide variety of God-created feelings in a way that makes the person functionally effective for the given situation and does not dishonor God. In this definition, the body, mind and spirit are working harmoniously together in a functional way. Of course, this ideal is not easily attained.

It is lamentable that mental/emotional wholeness has not been a priority for the majority of people. Over the years of my life I have interviewed hundreds of people with the following question: Did you ever learn from your parents or your school teachers the way to achieve emotional balance? And in almost every case, the answer was in the negative.

Millions of parents spend millions of dollars to ensure the medical, physical, intellectual development of their children but hardly ever a dollar or an hour of time to deal with emotional health. I know of hundreds of Christians who are physically healthy, intellectually erudite and morally upright but emotionally, they are severely impaired. Not surprisingly when a crisis event strikes suddenly, such otherwise well balanced and affable human beings collapse under the enormity of the emotional disequilibrium created. Hence the urgency of addressing mental/emotional wholeness.

To understand emotional wholeness we need to recognize that all emotions have validity. One must not make the mistake of demonizing an emotion because it has normatively negative associations. For example, the emotion of anger is perceived by some as totally dysfunctional. This view is not biblically correct. It is God, the Creator who equipped humanity with the great range of emotional experiences. The God who has blessed us with the emotion of happiness is the same God who has formed us in such a way that we can feel anger and fear. Any effort to suggest that a person should suppress a particular emotion can actually cause the person to become more dysfunctional and pave the way for even greater crises.

My position is not the negation of emotions but the healthy management of emotions. Emotional wholeness implies the proper understanding of the dynamics of emotional arousal and the functional management of any emotion that has legitimacy. A word of reservation is in order here: I do not think that anybody is actually capable of perfect emotional wholeness only because no one is ever totally free from the carnal nature.

Anger

To illustrate the point let me use an example involving the emotion of anger. John is at home glued to his big screen television, experiencing the emotion of happiness as he cheers for his favorite baseball team that happens to be winning. He is happy and excited because his team is winning. His happiness is solely the emotional response to his team's outstanding performance. Behaviorally, he screams with delight and yells with great exuberance and jumps up and down as another home run is scored. The phone rings. He is too engaged in this game to answer it so he lets it ring until he hears his wife's voice as she tries to leave a message on the answering machine. He runs to the phone and his wife informs him that she is at a police precinct a few miles away from home because she has just crashed his new car. John explodes with a torrent of obscene words and expletives as he curses his wife for smashing his new car. How is this possible? What accounts for this sudden transformation? What has changed to effect such a drastic emotional and behavioral outburst?

Such an outburst on the part of John is evidence of his lack of emotional maturity. It is very probable that he never was taught the importance of emotional wholeness and the methodology to acquire it. So he begins with a serious disadvantage. Lack of knowledge and lack of discipline is a deadly combination that can predispose people to be crisis prone.

In John's case, the thought of his new car being smashed evokes pain, the loss of something he cherishes. This thought pattern almost instantly evokes feelings of anger and rage, which, in turn, provoke him to destructive behavior. Whereas, before the phone call, he was experiencing exhilaration as a direct result of his team's victorious play, he now is aware of new information which is unpleasant. Thus he transfers the new external environment into the internal environment, his mind, and unthinkingly reacts to the negative thought environment in a way that potentially can create a crisis in his spiritual life, emotional life and his marriage. Thus the crisis is self-induced. He may argue that the crisis was the result of his wife's "crazy incompetence" but the real truth that he prefers to not confront is that he lacks self-control. The continuation of a lack of self-control would eventually destroy him and his marriage and, worst of all, his spiritual relationship with God.

The above scenario is one that is played out millions of times every day across the world because millions of people were never taught the principles of emotional wholeness. They have not been taught the legitimacy of, and the mechanisms to deal with, anger, grief, disappointment, guilt, hate, fear, worry, frustration, sorrow, bitterness, envy, pride and depression. All of these are emotions or symptoms of emotions that every human needs to understand and develop mastery over with the passage of time. The failure to deal effectively with these areas of life has led to immeasurable suffering mentally, emotionally, physically and spiritually. Exacerbating the problem is the impoverished spiritual lives of most people. Therefore they are not spiritually equipped to deal with such emotions which often lead to sinful behavior thus precipitating even greater and more severe crises for themselves and others in the society.

Temperament

In the matter of understanding emotional wholeness and the critical role it plays in preventing or minimizing crisis events it is vital for individuals to understand their emotional makeup. In fact, the more we understand ourselves in terms of our emotional strengths and weaknesses the better we are able

43

to cope with circumstances or to be alert to avoid situations which would involve a crisis situation for ourselves.

For example, if a person knows that he is emotionally better equipped to deal with tasks than with people it may be wiser for that person to spend more time with tasks than with people. If on the other hand a person has very little love for tasks but great passion for interaction with people then such a person is better suited to an environment that would facilitate social interaction.

The point here is that oftentimes people set themselves up for a crisis event by a failure to understand and act within their particular emotional constitution. In essence, I am talking about the need for all people to understand the dynamics of temperament and personality.

Often, I have counseled married couples who are engaged in major conflict to the point where separation is being considered. They are convinced that the marriage is not workable because they simply can no longer deal with their differences in style and emotional response to different stimuli. It is always amazing to note how these very same couples after understanding the theory of temperament and personality come to see that their crisis did not have to occur and that their marriage is salvageable.

In these cases and thousands of others the reason for the marriage crisis was the failure to understand and accept the different temperaments of the partners. Florence Littauer captures the core of the problem by writing that, *"without an understanding of the basic temperaments and the desires and needs of each, we tend to spend much of our time trying to get from other people responses that they just can't give. Many marriages for example come to a grinding halt because neither partner knows what the other wants or needs. With no simple tool to use, success is an accident. Once we begin to understand the basic desire of each nature, however, the veil is lifted and we have the key to getting along with others."*[xxiv]

Drs. Richard & Phyllis Arno define temperament as, *"the inborn part of man that determines how he reacts to people, places and things. In short, it is how people interact with*

44

their environment and the world around them. Temperament pinpoints our perception of ourselves and the people who love us. It is also the determining factor in how well we handle the stresses and pressures of life.[xxv] According to temperament theory people often experience interpersonal and intrapersonal conflicts when they attempt to meet their temperament needs in an ungodly way or when the temperament needs are out of balance or when they react negatively to unmet temperament needs. When an individual is not in harmony with his temperament needs or predisposition then such a person may he headed for an emotional crisis. How does this happen?

Researchers have identified five basic types of temperaments. They are melancholy, sanguine, choleric, supine and phlegmatic. These are all created by God and none is superior to another. God, in His wisdom created all types for the completion of His purposes for kingdom work. They all have their unique strengths and weaknesses. The problem is that most people are not aware that God designed people to be emotionally different in responses to environmental stimuli, especially in relationships. We are not to be all yellow pencils.

The tragedy is that in general, each person tends to evaluate the other by his own standards emotionally and otherwise. Therefore a sanguine person expects his spouse to perceive life through sanguine eyes. The problem is that his spouse may be melancholy. They are headed for a major crisis that can lead to divorce all because they failed to understand the God-created temperamental differences.

Perhaps a real case study would help to crystallize the significance of temperamental differences in creating a crisis condition and the effects upon people when they come to understand the reason for their conflicts.

I will use the case of Ralph and Linda (not their real names). Ralph and Linda wanted to get married as the fires of romance heated up and they knew that it was time for marriage. I cautioned them about their observable serious temperamental differences and the probable conflicts that would ensue. They seemed indifferent to such caution for they were madly in love. I knew a major crisis was in the making.

Shortly after marriage the problems began. Of course, they did not inform me because they were ashamed. But as the crisis worsened to the point where they actually had a short separation Linda called to set up an appointment. After listening to Linda's story it was obvious that what I had initially suspected was the real core of the conflict. So I requested that they permit me to do a temperament analysis on them. They agreed and we proceeded to have the profile done.

When I carefully reviewed the profiles with them I saw the essence of the problem and the reason for their heated conflict and dysfunctional behaviors. Ralph scored as a phlegmatic choleric in inclusion, phlegmatic melancholy in control and supine in affection. Linda scored phlegmatic choleric in inclusion, choleric in control and sanguine compulsive in affection. Since they did not understand and accept their natural differences they had been verbally fighting frequently.

As I began to interpret to them the essential differences in terms of thinking and behaving based on their different temperaments, they began to see why they both were unfulfilled in the marriage and why they had been thinking of separation. Their major problem was in the area of control and affection. Compounding the issue was their immature spiritual condition which exacerbated their relationship conflicts. Neither was prepared to meet the need of the other until each had his or her own needs met.

As I write they are still living in major disequilibrium because they both refuse to face up to their serious spiritual inadequacies. Lamentably, the husband does not even wish to receive any counsel because he does not think that he needs any help. His position is that Linda needs help. Unless they both invite the transforming presence of the Holy Spirit then their temperamental differences will cause them much pain and unnecessary anguish for the future.

This is only one of several examples of couples that have damaged each other by a failure to understand and accept the legitimate temperamental differences. In every case that I have worked with either one partner or both have allowed these differences to become points of major conflict and facilitated the work of Satan in causing them to engage in sinful behavior.

It is my belief that many couples would be spared the crisis event if they would make time to understand their own temperaments and that of their mates and then avail themselves of The Holy Spirit to function in an emotionally wholesome and spiritually holy manner. The advantage of a temperament profile is to get a picture of oneself emotionally and therefore be alert to one's weaknesses before a conflict situation arises. Of course, there is much more about temperament and personality but I consider this sufficient for the purpose intended in this book.

The Body-Mind-Spirit Connection

Hundreds of years of research have aptly demonstrated that emotions affect the physical health. The Holy Bible has long established this significant connection between the condition of one's health and the state of one's mind and emotions. In Proverbs 15:13 we read that *"a happy heart makes the face cheerful but heartache crushes the spirit"*.

Today, psychologists, secular and Christian concur but may use different terminology. A condition of emotional disequilibrium will soon lead to physical disequilibrium. Proverbs 14:30 uses even more powerful language to establish the mind-body connection. We read, *"A heart at peace gives life to the body but envy rots the bones"*.

Jesus Christ, the Incarnation of God, the greatest Teacher and the best Counselor, provided much knowledge which impacts upon emotional and spiritual wholeness. Oftentimes, he spoke of the need to forgive from the heart, those who offend us.

This is a spiritual matter and perhaps should be placed under the section on "Spiritual Wholeness" but the truth is that it is also relevant to the mind-body connection in regards to emotional and physical health. The Gospel writer, Matthew records for us an incident in which Peter had questioned Christ about how often he should forgive his brother.

And Peter confidently responded to his own question by suggesting, "up to seven times." Jesus then replied, *"I do not say to you, up to seven times, but up to seventy times seven."* The implication was, of course, that there is no numerical limitation on forgiveness. This is a very difficult demand upon us.

Not only is this a spiritual requirement but additionally, if more people practiced the principle of forgiveness, they would suffer less emotional disturbances and the consequent ill effects of emotional poison upon their bodies and minds and spirit.

Numerous diseases are the result of harboring hatred,

anger and bitterness in our emotional bank. After a certain amount of time, the build up of such negatives within the mind produces harmful physiological changes within the body, which precipitate physical illnesses. But when we choose to forgive we release ourselves from the poison of unforgiveness, cleanse the system of the destructive emotions and allow for healing. Therefore, forgiveness is a powerful antidote to emotional and physical crises. This is a powerful example of the inherent integration of the body, mind/emotions and spirit.

The lamentable tragedy is that millions of people every year enter into severe crises and stay in the crisis condition because they refuse to live in harmony with the laws governing emotions and health. God's word cannot be mocked. It would be much wiser to believe God since He designed the human body, soul and mind with the capacity for emotional expression. But alas, we allow our sinful condition to dictate our emotional responses. So we will continue to pay a costly price for disregarding the very laws that the Creator has given for our equilibrium.

It is clear that the Holy Bible establishes for us a very potent method for the minimization of crisis events and the dysfunctional responses to such crises. Dr. McMillen observes, *"No one can appreciate so fully as a doctor the amazing percentage of human disease and suffering which is directly traceable to worry, fear, conflict, immorality, dissipation, and ignorance – to unwholesome thinking and unclean living. The sincere acceptance of the principles and teachings of Christ with respect to the life of mental peace and joy, the life of unselfish thought and clean living, would at once wipe out more than half the difficulties, diseases and sorrows of the human race. In other words, more than half of the present affliction of mankind could be prevented by the tremendous prophylactic power of actually living up to the personal and practical spirit of the real teachings of Christ.*

The teachings of Jesus applied to our modern civilization-understandingly applied, not merely nominally accepted-would so purify, uplift and vitalize us that the race would immediately stand out as a new order of beings, possessing superior mental power and increased moral force. Irrespective of the future rewards of living, laying aside all discussion of future life, it would pay any man or woman to live the Christ-life for the mental and moral rewards it affords here in this present world. Some day our boasted scientific development, as regards mental and moral improvement, may indeed catch up with the teachings of this man of Galilee". [xxvi]

6. Spiritual Wholeness

Thus far in my presentation I have examined how crises can be significantly minimized, and in several instances, prevented if people would be willing to discipline themselves in the matter of the physical and the emotional. But wholeness is not complete until the spiritual component is addressed. I submit that this dimension is the most important area that counselors. Pastors and other helping professionals should address in helping clients to deal with existing crises and in preventing other crises later on in life.

Further, it is the spiritual that is the most powerful in shaping people's responses to crisis events about which I shall deal in the next chapter. If it were possible to develop the physical and emotional dimensions to perfection crises would still occur because the fact of life is that far too often, the crises experienced by millions of people have their roots in spiritual problems. Hence wholeness is only attainable in the proper integration of all three dimensions.

In speaking of the spiritual I think it necessary to define and clarify the meaning of "spirit". All humans, in spite of religious belief systems have been created with what the Bible calls, the spirit in man. So, Christians, Jews, Muslims, Hindus and indeed every other religious type possesses the human spirit. Therefore, it is practical to speak of the spiritual to people of all religions since they do have a connection to God through this spirit.

However, until one is regenerate by receiving the Holy Spirit, one cannot really experience spiritual wholeness and pursue true holiness. Holiness has meaning only in the context of seeking to be conformed to the image of Christ and letting Christ dwell within a person.

Holiness is never the product of moral rectitiude but rather, the active indwelling presence of the Holy Spirit, which implies that the old body of sin is dead and a new birth has taken place. This new birth cannot be effected without the Holy Spirit. Thus, for non-Christians a counselor may counsel concerning moral integrity and the development of the human spirit but cannot go much further unless the person is willing to enter into a living relationship with Jesus Christ and be sanctified by the Holy Spirit.

The new birth is required. This new birth means that the person now is able to mortify the deeds of the flesh by the Holy Spirit. The flesh is powerless against the sinful nature. Any holiness produced by the flesh is not authentic holiness. Authentic holiness is the work of the Holy Spirit. The Christian is one who is led by the Holy Spirit so that Christ may be fully formed in him.

Spiritual Abuse

Spiritual crises, which as we have ascertained can lead to emotional and physical crises, can be minimized by fellowship with a biblically sound and healthy congregation. Thousands of Christians are on a course to a major spiritual crisis by reason of their association with congregations that may be deemed as fringe, peripheral, cultic or heretical. Such worshippers are in danger of grave spiritual abuse that may leave them scarred for life emotionally and spiritually. Even worse, they may end up dead while acting under the instructions of their demonically inspired leaders.

This is a matter of historical documentation and current reality. Tens of thousands of seekers have, unfortunately, become the victims of false prophets, self-proclaimed apostles and messengers of God, apocalyptic leaders, and other such ministers of Satan.

Dr. Ronald Enroth, in his excellent book, *"Churches That Abuse"*, expounds the way in which religious people can become victims of major spiritual crisis and the subsequent negative emotional effects upon such.

As he puts it, *"Unlike physical abuse that often results in bruised bodies, spiritual and pastoral abuse leaves scars on the psyche and soul. It is inflicted by persons who are accorded respect and honor in our society by virtue of their role as religious leaders and models of spiritual authority. They base*

52

that authority on the Bible, the Word of God, and see them-selves as shepherds with a sacred trust. But when they violate that trust, when they abuse their authority, and when they mis-use ecclesiastical power to control and manipulate the flock, the results can be catastrophic. The perversion of power that we see in abusive churches disrupts and divide families, fos-ters an unhealthy dependence of members on the leadership, and creates, ultimately, spiritual confusion in the lives of the victims. "[xxvii]

Spiritually abusive churches and groups do exist, more than we may think. And tragically, millions have suffered severe spiritual crises because of their involvement in such. Leaders of such abusive groups routinely use fear, guilt, and intimidation as effective weapons to control their members. In fact, they foster an unhealthy dependence upon the leadership in spiritual, emotional, relational and even mundane matters.

The leaders feed the membership a steady diet of mes-sages focusing on themes of submission, loyalty, obedience to those in authority, exclusivism in relationships, and divine wrath for failure to follow the leaders. The members are promised exclusive rewards and are persuaded to believe that their relationship with God is unique among all humans.

Worse yet, the leaders of such cults and fringe sects deify themselves as specially appointed messengers of God who are His uniquely chosen representatives on earth. And so they actually brainwash naïve and unsuspecting religious types into accepting a totalitarian environment.

What are the dangers inherent in such groups? Clearly, while these people are in good standing with such groups they do not even recognize the extent to which they have given up their free will. Their very being is existent upon the "grace" of the leader. They are unknowingly in an unwholesome dependency relationship in which their emotions are only right as determined by the leader.

Their eternal salvation is at stake. And they will remain infantile in their mental, intellectual, emotional and spiritual development. Since their worth and esteem is a function of their faithfulness and loyalty to the group they are often forced to break family ties with those who disagree with them. Thus families are fractured and lives are thrown into permanent disequilibrium. It is no surprise that such people, as has happened in several documented cases, set dates for the return of Jesus and disconnect from this earthly existence to await the arrival of Jesus.

Worse yet, some have chosen to go meet Him by committing suicide leaving in their wake thousands of grieving and traumatized relatives and friends. What a travesty of humanity when humans virtually sell themselves to the power of a demented "spiritual" leader!

Should such people discover their mistakes before it is too late and choose to leave they still have a major spiritual and emotional crisis. I know of hundreds of people who having been involved in cultic "Christian" churches give up all faith in any church and even in the reality of Jesus Christ as Savior and Lord. It is a crisis of incredibly grave proportions when a human who once had a passion for spiritual things becomes embittered against Christianity and the very God of the Universe. But it is easy to understand the dynamics of this response.

When a person walks away from a legalistic, controlling, guilt-inducing and highly manipulative church, that person has not walked away from the damaging residual emotional and spiritual effects of the unhealthy relationship. He has to deal with huge emotional wounds, intense emotional pain and shameful memories that can haunt him for several years.

Some choose to deal with such a heavy load by leaving the spiritual arena of life completely and reject all religion. In fact, they can become so secular and materialistic that it seems like a totally different person has emerged. Well, yes! Such over compensative behavior is not uncommon among those who have suffered the agony of spiritual abuse. It is their way of making up for lost time and avoid the potential of more spiritual abuses. I personally know numerous people who fit this category.

Thousands of others do not wish to give up faith altogether in Jesus Christ. But they are in severe disequilibrium spiritually and emotionally. They need help to bring closure to their crisis, remove the emotional confusion, restore right relationships, regain the capacity for independent thinking and judgments, cope with disorientation and renew or develop, perhaps, for the very first time, a wholesome personal relationship with God. The truth is recovery from spiritual abuse is not easy for many. Such people urgently need to find a healthy, non-abusive, compassionate, caring, group of believers in which they may receive the healing that is needed. And even that search may be difficult because spiritual deception is a part of the fallen sinful condition of mankind. But the path to restoration is not impossible.

I believe that I can write on this subject of spiritual abuse with a real heart for it based not solely on academic and theological studies but rather based on my own journey within a Christian church that was, for decades, spiritually abusive. It was difficult to even leave the organization for fear that I would be sentenced to hell. So I stayed for years dealing with daily crises in my innermost being as I witnessed many being victimized by those in authority. By God's divine intervention I eventually departed. It was not shocking that many who wanted to leave justified their stay by reasoning that it was God's will for them to stay in such an abusive environment. And even though that particular denomination has become more orthodox in their doctrines and practices yet many bear the deep scars upon their souls. Thousands who left have become spiritual wanderers afraid of committing themselves to any religious group for fear of reliving the anguish and confusion.

On the subject of spiritual crisis it is very instructive to note that in 1999 numerous secular and religious authorities (or are they?) were predicting the collapse of society and the end of the world. As happened one thousand years ago when Christians and others precipitated major spiritual and emotional crises in their lives as a consequence of their mistaken conviction that Jesus was about to return a similar crisis was in the making. As we all now know, there was no computer collapse, no major malfunction of anything and no return of Jesus. Yet thousands of people made millions of dollars capitalizing on the fears and immaturity of millions of people. Ministers of religion were, in some cases, actually pressuring their own people and others to get ready for the return of Jesus by selling all their stuff and move out to other areas. Others were encouraged to stockpile food and essential equipment to ensure their survival.

It was a crisis for some. I thank God that the majority of people were sane enough to not make rash decisions. But such a situation and others that will follow as we move through the first few years of this new century demonstrates the tendency of people to be victims of crises in religious matters. Christians can prevent such crises if they pursue wholeness and holiness as rightly discerned through historic theological orthodoxy, scripturally accurate psychology and experiential wisdom in harmony with the Holy Bible. Jesus Christ Himself warned the Church against such spiritual abuses. Tragically many Christians are not diligent students of The Holy Bible and are unable to distinguish the counterfeit from the authentic. Watchful Christians can avert a personal spiritual disaster by sticking to the Holy Bible rather than by following the alarmists and mercenaries who make merchandise of naïve people.

Even though the Y2K mania is over it may be instructive for the future to consider an article run by Newsday, a highly recognized newspaper, in January 1999. *"Pilgrims have come to Jerusalem for thousands of years, but as the Christian calendar millennium approaches, the pilgrims' fervor is growing. So called "end-timers" with varying visions of an impending apocalypse, are making their way to this stony hilled city where the Bible says Jesus was crucified and resurrected."*[xxviii] Further in this article, evidence is provided for the influx of visitors into Israel. Many of these people are cultists who are extreme in their beliefs and practices and who often foment the spiritual crises for people. It is no surprise that, *"many new hoteliers are gearing up for the flood of visitors. Thousands of new hotel rooms are being built, and*

Israel's tourism ministry has launched an advertising blitz to remind people of the city's millennial significance. One hotel sent out fliers to 2,000 Christian groups that read: How would you like to be staying at the Mount of Olives Hotel the day Jesus returns? .....Some psychiatrists here expect an increase in the number of cases of "Jerusalem Syndrome" which they describe as a temporary insanity that lasts about a week and affects visitors who otherwise have never shown any signs of mental illness. "xxix

It is my prayer and hope that people would have learned the lesson from this experience. But the lesson of history is that people do not learn from history. It seems that another generation will be doomed to make the same mistakes of the previous generation. I urge you to stay in touch with the revelation of God as recorded for humanity in the pages of the Bible and not follow after extremists, alarmists, psychics, self appointed prophets, and those who claim to have special access to secret knowledge.

Sexual Sins

A major problem of every human being until conquered by God is the pursuit of happiness as more desirable than the pursuit of holiness. Whenever happiness becomes a priority over holiness then crises would follow. Happiness is essentially the emotional response to a given situation and since most people desire happiness they would often engage in behavior that may be sinful. The anticipation of pleasure drowns out the fear of sinning. In other words, the pleasure principle is more powerful in the lives of most people than the holiness principle. The pursuit of pleasure is considered a greater reason for living than the pursuit of holiness. In the process of pursuing pleasure the spirit in man is starved, God is dishonored, Satan is worshiped, the flesh is gratified and mankind enters into deeper darkness. The lamentable truth is that most people are currently living a morally and spiritually deficient lifestyle that makes them prone to experience major crises.

Let us examine the matter of sexual sin to elucidate the point. God is very clear about His position on sexual matters. Both the Old Testament and the New Testament warn against sexual immorality, which includes fornication, adultery, homosexuality, bestiality, incest, pornography, and a host of other sexual aberrations. But mankind has spurned God's spiritual laws. And what a price society has paid. History is replete with major crises in the lives of great men and women, who by their rebellion against the laws of holiness, have precipitated national and international crises. Almost every one knows the story of the Noatian deluge that God sent upon a world that had forsaken His laws regarding sex and other related matters. And almost everyone knows the horrible story of the destruction of Sodom and Gommorrah, the twin cities of sin. Here were two cities saturated with every sexual perversion possible. They suffered the ultimate crisis, the annihilation of their cities and the death of all save Lot, his wife and two daughters.

Today, America is plagued with millions of lives in crisis because of sexual sin. And the reasons are very obvious. Even a casual observation of most bookstores, magazine stands, video stores, television movies and Internet sites tell the sordid story. We are a nation given over to every imaginable sexual lust and perversion. It is no surprise that millions of people are reaping the negative effects of worshipping sex rather then the God who created sex. These negative effects are manifest in divorce, fractured families, emotional trauma for cheated spouses, dysfunctional behavior in children of broken families, abortions, sexually transmissible diseases and a host other horrible consequences.

Let me explain the dynamics of a crisis created by sexual sin by examining a typical example of teenage pregnancy. When a teenage girl becomes pregnant outside marriage and has to decide on abortion of the child or letting the child live that is a crisis. If she keeps the child then her life is thrown into significant disequilibrium. She may have to quit school, find employment, may be expelled from her parents home, may be abandoned by her boyfriend and may eventually end up as millions of other girls, an impoverished single mother who must depend on welfare to get just the basics of life. At the worst, she may have to resort to prostitution to earn her living or commit suicide to avoid all the shame and pain.

But it is not just the girl who lives in this crisis condition. The parents of this girl now face a major crisis, as they must make major decisions. If they choose to keep their daughter and her child their lives are thrown into disequilibrium because they were not planning for a baby in the family. The siblings of the girl are thrown into a crisis because they now have to compete with a new person in the family. And what about the child who is born without a father and the sanctity of the family as ordained by God? In most cases that child is a crisis waiting to happen. And most likely, if this child grows to become an adult, she would make the same mistake and the cycle only continues from generation to generation. What a price to pay for a moment of sexual pleasure!

The above scenario is not just my imagination going crazy. The tragic truth is that the thousands are playing out the above scenario every day in this nation. The statistics are shocking as this nation continues to reject the spiritual dimension of wholeness. Sin carries a very high price tag, higher than most people can pay. And yet as a nation, we skirt the real issues, justify and rationalize sexually promiscuous behavior. In fact, we prefer avoid the term "sin". The "authorities" propose the teaching of safe sex, the easy availability of contraceptives and the rights of teens to receive medical care without parental knowledge. The only "safe sex" is the one commanded by God. Any sex outside the parameters defined by the Holy God is not safe! God's word will not be mocked. If people want to avoid the crisis of sexual sins then they must stay away from the sin.

Abortions

Consider the enormity of crisis with regard to the fact of abortions in this nation. It is well known among sociologists, psychologists and other professional helpers that since the U.S. Supreme Court legalized unrestricted abortion in the infamous Roe v. Wade battle in January 1973, almost 38 million abortions have been performed. In 1973, 744,600 abortions were performed. In 1997 the number rose to 1.2 million. The figure of 38 million is staggering to the imagination. Do we stop to reflect that such a figure means that millions of women experienced a major crisis of conscience as they debated abortion or not? What about the fathers of the aborted babies, the parents of the pregnant woman, the siblings of the pregnant girls and the friends who may be negatively impacted? Do we understand that such a mind-boggling number involves crises of every description and intensity, legal, financial, medical, social, emotional, mental, spiritual? Do we understand that millions of women have been permanently damaged emotionally and, in many cases, physically?

Those who have actually experienced the trauma of abortion have admitted that their lives are never the same after the event. Psychologists use the term, post abortion syndrome, to encapsulate the emotional devastation that such women often experience for several years after the actual abortion. They live with emotional detachment and suffer tremendous guilt. Some find it almost impossible to forgive themselves or believe that God would forgive such a horrible act.

In addition to this emotional and spiritual nightmare they often have difficulty in later pregnancies. In fact some are never able to carry a full term baby and so must face the trauma of never having a child through natural means. And yet, with this information available, the government of this nation continues to support abortions. Once again, we see the folly of humanity and the reason for dysfunctional lifestyles.

Is the crisis of abortion preventable? Of the 38 million abortions, unmarried women obtained 31 million. Did God not forbid premarital sexual relationships? Had these women (and men who were responsible for the impregnation of the women) obeyed God's law on sexuality then 31 million abortions would have been avoided.

Sexual Diseases

The statistical information concerning the numbers of people suffering from sexual diseases is staggering to the imagination. In a recent article carried in Newsday it was reported that *"The number of cases of sexually transmitted diseases in the U.S. has risen by several million in the eight year period from 1988-1996, but experts say the increase is due mostly to better reporting".*[xxx] The experts may choose to argue the actual trends in terms of numbers but it does not change the fact that millions of Americans are suffering crises that are the result of sexual sins. The same article continued by giving some really alarming statistical data. *"A study by a panel of health experts has found that approximately 15.3 million cases of sexually transmissible diseases – such as chlamydia, gonorrhea and syphilis – occurred in the United States in 1996 in contrast to 12 million cases in 1988. The panel estimated that 45 million Americans have herpes, 20 million have HPV or genital warts, 750,00 have hepatitis B, and 560,000 have HIV. All four of these diseases infect people for life but other STD's are curable".*[xxxi]

I can write much about each one of these sexual diseases but I think that writing about just one would suffice. I will deal with the rapidly increasing incidence of AIDS that has already killed over 16 million people, worldwide. And the most tragic part is that this crisis could have been totally prevented. For the most part AIDS is a fully preventable crisis except in those cases where a child is born with AIDS because the parents carry the virus. Of course, if parents are living lives within the culture of holiness it is highly improbable that they would contract this deadly disease. Therefore it would be highly improbable that their offspring would be afflicted with this deadly disease.

AIDS is a powerful case for the pursuit of wholeness and holiness. God has ordained certain moral laws to govern life. When those laws are transgressed there is a price spiritually, emotionally and, in some cases, physically. The statistics on AIDS are mind boggling. Literally, millions of people have invited a major crisis into their lives by living a lifestyle contrary to holiness. The consequences of AIDS are enormous not simply because people die prematurely, but even more destabilizing is the impact upon the millions of children who are left without parents. These children are doomed to grow up with major emotional, psychological and spiritual crises. Such children, particularly, if they live in the impoverished nations of the earth, may never have the opportunity to receive a solid education and proper medical care. Essentially, short of a miracle, they are doomed to a life of misery until death.

Consider the statistical information as reported in Newsday, Tuesday, Nov. 24th 1998. *"Worldwide the HIV pandemic grew by millions this year, driven by new infections in people aged 10 to 24 years. In that group, five people were infected every minute in 1998, says a UN report. The HIV epidemic continues to expand at a staggering pace, particularly among teenagers and post-adolescent adults in the poorer countries of the world. Nearly half of all new HIV infections this year – 5.8 million – occurred in people aged 10 to 24 years."[xxxii]*

Newsweek magazine of January 17, 2000 ran its cover story article on AIDS in Africa. The tragedy unfolding in Africa is of such magnitude that it is, I think, impossible to grasp its severity unless one is an actual witness to the immeasurable suffering. According to this article, *"The global death toll from Aids was 2.6 million last year alone. Roughly 85 percent of those deaths occurred in Africa. Even as the corpses were buried, some 5.6 million more people- mostly African- became infected with HIV during 1999. ...By the end of this year, an astonishing 10.4 million African children under 15 will have lost their mothers or both parents to AIDS- 90 percent of the global total of AIDS orphans.[xxxiii]*

While the majority of these deaths and current cases of infection and orphans are not in North America, the fact of the matter is that millions of human beings, who are created in the image and likeness of God, are living in a crisis situation every day because they were not educated to live the lifestyle of wholeness and holiness. Even more worrisome and damaging is their potential to infect other millions with each passing year. In most of these cases, the victims are not even aware of God's laws of holiness. But in many, particularly, here in the US, the victims are very much aware of God's laws regarding sexual immorality but do not really respect God. The pursuit of carnal pleasure is, for them, of greater value than the honor of God. Whether one contracts the deadly disease of AIDS or any of the sexually transmissible diseases for lack of knowledge or for the pursuit of pleasure in spite of knowing God's laws, the fact remains that millions of people are living in a crisis condition which could have been avoided. For some, they are able to regain some significant degree of equilibrium, while for many, life is a permanent state of disequilibrium as they await a horrible death.

Such data should be enough reason for massive campaigns in morality training and spiritual holiness. While governmental and social agencies are handing out more condoms, even to school students, the crisis of sexual diseases and its traumatic emotional effects widens and intensifies by the millions. It is obvious that the secular sociologists, psychologists, humanists and the politicians have failed miserably in their efforts to hold back the rushing tide of sexual diseases. It should be clear that what is needed urgently is a concerted campaign to teach all children and all adults that spiritual wholeness and holiness are major factors in crisis prevention. The answer is not more condoms or more drugs, or more funds for research. If we want to prevent the destructive onslaught of tens of millions of lives then there needs to be a turning to God and His laws of holiness.

My position on the way to minimize the crises created by sexual sins is unequivocal. Spending billions of dollars in research to cure AIDS and other sexually transmissible diseases will not solve the crisis. Funding the distribution of free contraceptives to sexually active teens will not resolve the crisis.

Promoting educational efforts that legitimize the gay or lesbian lifestyles will not free society from the crisis. Attempting to use humanistic education to promote "good" values has no power to prevent sexual immorality. All such efforts are misguided and doomed to ultimate failure.

So, what can be done? Channel the billions of dollars into educational institutions, high schools, colleges, universities, community centers and churches. Equip these institutions with Christian counselors, Christian pastors, Christian social workers and Christian teachers who would be empowered to teach our children and young adults the path to crisis minimization by the pursuit of wholeness and holiness.

I ask the question: Were these crises, by the millions preventable? And the answer is a resounding. "yes". Tragically, our society has rejected the development of the moral and spiritual. The belief in Jesus Christ is not fashionable. Holiness is not considered as a viable alternative or a desirable lifestyle. Spiritual matters are sacrificed on the altars of sexual pleasure, sensual indulgences, fleshly gratification, material acquisition and monetary remuneration. Hollywood, sports, entertainment and the shopping malls are the new gods to be worshiped. Millions spend their time, their money, and their energy on the highway to crisis and eternal death.

Simple obedience to God's laws governing all sexual relationships would prevent the millions of illegitimate babies, the millions of abortions and the millions of sex addicts who live with unhealthy obsessions. Imagine for a moment a society living according to God's laws forbidding sexual immorality. Within one year hundreds of millions of crises, worldwide, would be prevented. Within a few years the whole structure of society would be radically transformed so that a crisis would be an abnormal event rather than the norm.

Divorce

I think it would be terribly lacking to speak of crisis and not address the subject of divorce. I have chosen to place this topic here cognizant of the fact that divorce is a crisis event and simultaneously, the response to other crises in lives of dysfunctional couples. Divorce is a plague of major proportions. In 1994 1.2 million marriages were ended in divorce by rule of law. As we enter a new century the rate of divorce has risen to 50 percent. This means that for every two marriages there is one divorce. The statistics tell only a tiny part of the real crisis produced by divorce. The cost in human life as evidenced by broken families, delinquent children, runaway children prostitution, family impoverishment, domestic violence, emotional abuse, dysfunctional blended families, sibling rivalry, second and third marriages, criminal behavior, sexual abuse, and a host of other unspecified effects is incalculable. The crisis of divorce if left unresolved will destroy an entire nation. It is perhaps the most critical factor in the moral and spiritual collapse of the country. The crisis of divorce with its attendant evils is like a bulldozer destroying everything in its path. And the tragedy only worsens as humanity continues to reject the revealed laws governing marriage. How tragic that we have entered into such spiritual darkness that divorce is now perceived as normal as burgers and fries while a marriage of many years is perceived as an aberration, a shock, and a strange thing!

The fact is that America's divorce rate is the highest in the world. The results upon the family have been extremely tragic. It is now estimated that a total of 20 million children live with single parents. Consider for a few moments the repercussions for the 20 million children when they become adults. The evidence suggests very clearly that these adults will continue in a path that will further destroy the family and create even greater disequilibrium for other millions that yet to be born. Here in America, as in several other countries, the family is danger of extinction. The time has come for all that love life and freedom to engage in a mission to save the family.

While theologians and others argue about the act of divorce as sin, I submit that divorce is the result of sin. It is the result of the sins of one partner or both. People have become too self-absorbed, too obsessed with self-fulfillment, too focused on self-satisfaction to truly love their spouses as God commands. It is this obsession with self that destroys relationships and leads to divorce. Whereas Jesus teaches self-denial and loving neighbor as self the culture of darkness glorifies the worship of self. The person who worships himself can hardly be expected to live with anyone who interferes with his/her self-image. Of course, we should know that the worship of self is idolatry and God declares that idolatry is sin!

The scholars may debate the issue until the return of Christ but that does not change the fact that the root cause of divorce is a spiritual crisis. People have forgotten, perhaps, conveniently that the Creator of the marriage institution has established laws to bind couples together. When we continuously expose ourselves to the selfishness and sensuality of modern culture as graphically depicted on modern television and the Internet it is no strange thing that we find our mates unattractive, unappealing and undesired. At such a point in the relationship it becomes difficult to practice the power of love. The emotional distance is already present and continues to grow being fueled by the illusion portrayed in the media. Before long one partner makes the decision that it is time to move to a new spouse. So marriage is perceived as a marketable commodity to be traded and used and resold. One wonders where is God in all of this. Does God have a right to speak on the matter of marriage and divorce? Does it not make sense that we humans should seek to listen to the One who created the family?

Yet another problem is that most people seeking marriage are not prepared to handle the dynamics of marriage in all of its complex implications and ramifications. In most cases, the couple does not even understand the real purpose of marriage. They have been misinformed by a decadent society and so they enter marriage with the wrong paradigms, erroneous expectations, false assumptions, and unhealthy habits. The result is divorce and remarriage and more divorce and remarriage while the culture of crisis and death exacts a heavy toll upon the whole society.

In one sense the crisis of divorce is the crisis of humanity in their relationship to God. Mankind has forsaken God and so it is no surprise that the quality of commitment that is vital for the endurance of any relationship is lacking in human relationships. Emotional immaturity fueled by passionate indulgences of the flesh leaves people empty. In forsaking God people have come to serve the created more than the Creator. It is essentially idolatry and idolatry is sin. Fulfillment cannot come from the worship of the created. Too often individuals seek a marriage partner who would fulfill all their physical, sexual, emotional and spiritual needs. This very infantile obsession with need fulfillment is at the root of failed marriages. The fulfillment of the void cannot be met by one marriage or the combination of several. Only when humans become fulfilled by God can they expect their marriages to make sense. And this can only happen when we put the pursuit of spiritual wholeness and holiness as the number one priority in out lives. Both the husband and wife need to understand and practice the glorification of God in the marriage relationship. When Jesus becomes the core of the marriage then divorce will not be an issue.

Christian counselors, educators and pastors have a vital role to play in the prevention or minimization of divorce. It is absolutely imperative that premarital education be offered and that such is followed up by further education after marriage. At the same time, couples have to take more responsibility for their actions and understand that they do have power to determine the level of crisis in their marriage. It is worth repeating that people need to understand that the adoption of any lifestyle has consequences. The lifestyle of self-gratification and fleshly fulfillment will lead to the crisis of divorce and all of its attendant pain, heartache, legal problems, financial crises, loneliness, custody of children, and perhaps, lead to alcohol and drug abuse or, even worse, suicide. The lifestyle of wholeness and holiness will lead to joy, peace and enduring love which would be a sweet aroma powerfully influencing the children produced in such a marriage for a wholesome life.

f. Covetousness

Yet another example of how obedience to God's laws of holiness would prevent crisis is in the matter of covetousness. Millions of people in America and, indeed, all over the world experience major financial and legal and emotional crises all because they disregard God's law which forbids covetousness. When God was establishing His covenant with Israel, He warned them, *"You shall not covet your neighbor's house. You shall not covet your neighbor's wife, or his manservant, or maidservant, his ox, or donkey, or anything that belongs to your neighbor."* Countless millions of humans have pierced themselves with immeasurable emotional devastation in their carnal desire to live a lifestyle which they could not legitimately afford and therefore proceeded to satiate their lustful desires by theft, gambling, embezzlement, tax fraud, illegal business operations, and other self destructive methods. When a human mind becomes fixated on some object of desire that mind would generate and justify a cognitive process and a corresponding course of action that defies conventional wisdom and the very laws of God and society in its passionate pursuit of the objective. The results are often tragic beyond belief.

The apostle Paul warns Christians against covetousness by identifying some of the disastrous consequences. What profound counseling wisdom as he instructs, *"But godliness with contentment is great gain. For we brought nothing into this world and we can take nothing out of it. But if we have food and clothing, we will be content with that. People who want to get rich fall into temptation and a trap and into many foolish and harmful desires that plunge men into ruin and destruction. For the love of money is a root of all kinds of evil. Some people, eager for money, have wandered from the faith and pierced themselves with many griefs."* **(I Timothy 6:6-10).** All the credit counselors, financial analysts, market consultants, and business executives together cannot provide better counseling than the words of Paul, the servant of God.

The consequences of breaking this law are evident all around. Thousands spend time in jail or in mental hospitals or in drug rehabilitation centers or declare bankruptcy or live in fear of the creditors and collection agencies because they chose to pursue a course of action guaranteed to produce crisis. We hear of thousands of people who are in great financial debt having used their credit cards to the limits and face the prospect of financial ruin and the resultant emotional pain associated with such. Why? Because they failed to obey a very simple law given by a very loving and wise God. This God commands, "Do not covet". It seems that millions of people are addicted to shopping almost totally oblivious of the fact of impending financial chaos. Unable to control their carnal desires to own more and more of that which does not truly satisfy they plunge themselves into disaster. They serve the created rather than the Creator and so their lives are prone to all types of crises. O! the wisdom of God as He provides humanity principles by which to live the full wholesome life. O! the folly of man to disregard the laws of this God.

I am constantly amazed at the multitudes that flock to the shopping malls of New York and of course all the cities across America. I often walk around just to look at people who have this compulsion to buy especially around certain holidays. It never ceases to astound me that the people who often complain of no time or money for the spiritual aspects of life find very generous portions of time and money to shop during the holidays These include New year's Day, Valentine's Day, President's Day, Easter, Mother's Day, Memorial Day, Father's Day, Independence Day, Labor Day, Thanksgiving and, of course, Christmas. These are the days when the shopping malls become the houses of worship. On Sundays the car parks of the churches are half-empty while the car parks of the malls are filled. From store to store they move with energy and passion. Their faces are aglow with excitement and happiness. Then the worshipper (shopper) finds his special object of devotion and quickly pulls out his credit card to make an offering unto the Lord (the manufacturer).

Have I exaggerated? You be the judge the next time you go to a shopping mall. Most people do not even realize their addiction to shopping. They derive a significant sense of worth, happiness and self-fulfillment to the degree that they can shop. They are like little children who find pleasure in the things they possess. And soon they become possessed by the things they own. They purchase more than they can ever use but their appetite for more grows with every new friend, fad, and fashion. The sad truth is that many people are in the grip of covetousness and do not even know it. These are the same people who will argue that they cannot find time to worship God. I wonder why. Is it that they have changed gods? Is it perhaps that they now worship the created thing rather the Creator?

Closely tied in with covetousness are pride and greed. These twin evils of pride and greed have been responsible for untold suffering for hundreds of millions of people down through the ages of human history. Millions of people have perished on the battlefields or suffered irreparable damage to their bodies. Hundreds of millions have lived in impoverished economic conditions because of rulers, kings, politicians and dictators who allowed their pride and greed to become their gods. Countless millions have been slaughtered on the altars of pride and greed, theirs or somebody else's. It is easy to sweep all this away with one brush of the hand and relegate this matter to historical folly and political miscalculations. But the truth is that even today millions of individuals are pursuing a course of thinking and behaving based on pride and greed that will land them in deep crisis.

The truth of the matter is that a sinful lifestyle would produce crisis events. The spiritual laws established by God cannot be violated without its penalty. It is the same with the physical laws that govern the universe. If a person chooses to jump off a high building he can only travel in one direction according to the law of gravity. And he will suffer serious injury or death as he hits the ground beneath the building. God has, in His love and wisdom, established spiritual laws that are intended for man's joy and peace. The infraction of His laws will incur pain and ultimately, death. On this matter, more counselors and pastors need to educate humans that sin is real and the consequences of sin are inevitable.

I think it is vital that Christians who are in a position of leadership within the church and community warn all people about the greatest crisis event any human can ever face is to stand before the judgment seat of God and be condemned to suffer eternal punishment. Every person who has lived or will ever live must come before the judgment seat of the Creator of the Universe. At such a critical moment nothing and nobody would be able to offer any help. All our friends in Hollywood, the White House, Wall Street, or anywhere in the corridors of power and wealth will be of no avail. No lawyer, politician, CEO, sports star, Oscar winner, oil tycoon, king, president, counselor, minister, evangelist or whoever will be of any help to anybody. On that day it will be the sole judgment of God and no one will be able to appeal to any higher authority.

Those of us who know Jesus Christ as personal Savior and Lord have the responsibility to witness to others so that they too may know Him. Those of you who are reading this book but do not know God must make a decision to face this eternal crisis or avoid this crisis. Christians have the opportunity to spread the love of God by helping as many as possible to come to know Jesus Christ and thus avert the most deadly and permanent crisis possible. In the chapter on "Implementation Of Model" I will suggest some possible ways to help our fellow brothers and sisters to develop lifestyles that are functional. We cannot take this responsibility lightly because the eternity of people is at stake. Surely if we are concerned about a person's physical health and emotional well being then we should be far more concerned about this person's spiritual condition now and for all eternity.

71

7: Minimizing the Crisis Response

In the previous section I examined the critical dimensions of wholeness in making the case for minimization of crises, or in many cases, the actual prevention of crises. One is not to assume then that if all of the rules were followed crisis would never occur. As I explained in the section on "The Inevitability of Crisis" crises are a part of the fallen condition of mankind. Crisis, at the very core, is simply the result of man's sinful condition and the curse placed upon the earth.

Let us suppose that the individual does all that is humanly possible to correctly integrate the physical (the body) and the mental/emotional (the soul) and the spiritual (the spirit) it is not absolutely guaranteed that he would be free from a crisis condition. God's sovereignty is still a most significant factor in the equation. And of course, accidents may occur, unforseen emergencies may suddenly arise, or unanticipated conditions may develop precipitating a crisis in our lives or the lives of our families and close friends. Thus it is not just a matter of living a lifestyle to prevent or minimize crisis.

The functionally whole human being must be prepared to deal with the exigencies of crisis events notwithstanding their particular origins or causative factors. Hence the need to address the matter of minimizing the dysfunctional response to crisis events.

When I say, "minimizing the crisis response" I do not imply that there would be no response. Rather, I am concerned with the minimization of negative or dysfunctional responses to crisis events. The fact is that every event, crisis or not, evokes a response. For some the response is functionally healthy, while for others, the response is dysfunctional and self destructive or other destructive. In theological language, the functional response would equate with a spiritual response while the dysfunctional response would equate with the carnal response. Tragically, the normal response to crisis events is carnal, of the flesh. People tend to simply react with the fleshly nature, which is in conflict with the divine nature.

Let me illustrate this by a case study. Brian returns

home very late one night and his wife, Betty, rebukes him for not calling her about his delay at the office. But Brian is really tired and wants to get some peace and rest. Feeling threatened and diminished by his wife he turns this minor crisis event into a major problem by responding to his troubled emotional state in a carnal way. He verbally abuses his wife. She responds in like manner and a very heated argument ensues. Overcome by anger they both allow the situation to get out of control. They hurl insults at each other even bringing up past mistakes that were supposed to have been buried.

Brian storms out of the house to find a place of solace. Under the control of anger he is unable to think intelligently and rationally. So he heads for the local bar where he can socialize with some of his regular friends and forget about his troubles at home.

Once he gets to the bar he begins the rite of imbibing alcohol. His friends encourage him to drink in order to get over the feelings of hurt and anger. His drinking continues until he becomes inebriated to the point where he is no longer in control of his emotions or behavior. And then an attractive lady whom he had met before comes to his side and offers to provide him some comfort. He accepts the proposition and finds himself waking up in the bed of a woman, not his wife. Eventually, he goes home and his wife discovers the truth of his previous night and he now finds himself in the midst of a real crisis which threatens his marriage, his family, his image and of course, his relationship with God. Could Brian have minimized this crisis response to the minor crisis event?

In the previous chapter, I explained how the pursuit of wholeness and holiness as a lifestyle model serves to minimize crises in the life of a person. Now, once again, I apply the twin principles of wholeness and holiness to explain how a person can minimize dysfunctional responses to crises.

Back to Brian and Betty. Let us allow for his negligence in failing to communicate with his wife of his unavoidable delay at the office. He returns late and his wife is upset. She is hurt because she perceives his failure to communicate with her about this delay as a lack of love and respect. She feels devalued and rather than seek to understand his situation she rebukes him for his inconsiderate behavior. What could have Brian done to minimize the crisis? Is there a way he could have minimized the negative response as described in the previous paragraph? Absolutely!

In the book of Romans chapter 12 verses 1 to 2 I find a powerful solution to crisis events. When properly understood and applied in the life of a Christian, dysfunctional responses to any crisis event would be minimized, if not totally avoided. Paul, the Apostle, writes, *"Therefore, I urge you, brothers, in view of God's mercy, to offer your bodies as living sacrifices, holy and pleasing to God-this is your spiritual act of worship. Do not conform any longer to the pattern of this world but be transformed by the renewing of your mind"*. From these verses I wish to extract two core principles for the pursuit of holiness which if followed as a lifestyle model, would prepare a person for responding spiritually to the crisis event. The first principle is: Do not conform to the pattern of this world. The second principle is: Be transformed by the renewing of your mind.

Do Not Conform to this World

I shall deal first with, "do not conform to the pattern of this world." God is here revealing for us that the normative approach to life is the wrong one. The world as a whole is under the influence of the devil, Satan. It is Satan's desire to see that no one receives salvation and therefore he will work to influence people to develop values, attitudes, behaviors that would keep people dysfunctional. The pattern established and followed in this world is essentially a sinful one even if most people do not like to use the term.

The Apostle John writing in **I John 2:15-16** helps us understand the pattern of this world by writing, *"Do not love the world or the things in the world. If anyone loves the world, the love of the father is not in him. For all that is in the world* **- the lust of the flesh, the lust of the eyes and the pride of life-** *is not of the Father but of the world."* Here, God is clearly showing that humans tend to respond to life's situations and circumstances from the perspective of the lust of the flesh, the lust of the eyes and the pride of life. Whenever a human responds to a crisis event on the basis of any of these three modes of operation then the response would certainly be a dysfunctional or sinful one which would in turn lead to an even greater crisis.

In the previous chapter, I explained how these three modes of operation cause millions of people to live a lifestyle that brings crises into their lives. If counselors and pastors and other Christian helpers could really impact this point upon people millions of crisis events would be prevented and billions of dollars would be available for the bona fide development of our civilization. Similarly, these three modes of operation must be understood in the matter of responding to a crisis. If the response to a crisis event were based upon the lust of the flesh or the lust of the eyes or the pride of life then the individual would become more dysfunctional as he moves into greater disequilibriumn.

So, in essence, the pattern of this world involves wrong thinking, which leads to wrong feeling, which leads to wrongdoing. For most people the problem is simply that their thought life is unholy. An unholy thought life naturally leads to an unholy feeling life, that is the magnification of harmful emotions. Sooner or later, the unholy feelings would lead to unholy behavior that the Creator calls, sin. Paul is therefore arguing the case for the Christian to reject the pattern of this world because the pattern of this world leads to a crisis prone life burdened with unhappiness, plagued by fear and guilt and worry and subject to eternal death.

Be Transformed

If then humans should not conform to the sinful pattern in the world to what and who should they conform? The answer to this question is the second core principle extracted from Romans 12:1-2, which is: Be transformed by the renewing of your mind. In this principle lies the very heart of the principle of the pursuit of holiness. God commands transformation! Transformation is much more than reformation. A reformed mind still possesses parts of the old because it is a matter of taking the old and doing some work on it. A transformed mind implies one that has been replaced by something else. And what will that something else be?

We note the latter part of verse 2 of Romans 12, ...Then you will be able to test and to approve what God's will is – His good, pleasing and perfect will. It seems then that Paul is asking Christians to seek the very mind of God. This is clarified for us when we go to **II Corinthians 3:18** which reads as follows, *"And we, who with unveiled faces all reflect the Lord's glory, are being transformed into His likeness with ever-increasing glory, which comes from the Lord, who is the Spirit."* Holiness is only possible when a person is equipped with the mind of Jesus Christ. Consider, for a moment, the implications for a person who has the perfect mind of Christ. This, of course, is the idealization of the concept of transformation. I think it helpful to look at the idealization to appreciate the power of this principle in the minimization of the crisis response. So let us look at Jesus, himself.

Did Jesus ever face any crisis event? Were his crisis events minor or major? How did he respond to the crisis events? In the answer to these questions I am convinced counselors will see the validity of my point that people can minimize dysfunctional responses to crises by the pursuit of holiness as an ongoing lifestyle. So back to the matter of crisis events in the life of the greatest example who ever walked upon this earth. It is not my intention to identify every crisis event in the life of Christ for I do not think such is necessary to establish my point. I have chosen what any Christian would consider the greatest crisis faced by Jesus, perhaps, the greatest crisis event any human could ever face! And that crisis which is really a series of crisis events is the betrayal, arrest, punishment and crucifixion of Jesus. Truly, there can be no greater example!

Ponder for a moment the typical human being facing denial and betrayal by trusted friends, slander, illegal arrest, mockings, scourgings, excruciatingly painful torture, public humiliation in the presence of family members and close friends and a journey to one's place of crucifixion. Such conditions will tax a person's physical, emotional and spiritual capacity to its limit. Here is a crisis of immeasurable magnitude. The typical response would be highly dysfunctional as the person seeks desperately to escape such horrible agony and prove his innocence.

Now consider how Jesus responded. He did not even raise his voice to condemn or ridicule his interrogators and tormentors. Amidst all the physical and emotional pain of this crisis, he maintained his composure and never sinned. In fact, as he lay dying upon the cross he even forgave his murderers. His crisis never impaired his emotional and spiritual wholeness even though his physical well being was impaired. Of course, this example is that of one who was God incarnate. No human can duplicate this remarkable level of wholeness. And indeed, no one is being called upon to become Jesus because no one can! The essential point for the human being is to recognize that spiritual transformation equips and fortifies an individual to face the crises of life in spite of the causes because the pursuit of holiness requires the indwelling presence of Jesus Christ in the sanctified individual.

The point of all this is to grasp the urgency of leaving the sinful nature and replacing it with the spiritual nature. The apostle, Paul, gives us penetrating insight and furnishes us with the right psychological dynamics when he declares that, *"Those who live according to the sinful nature have their minds set on what that nature desires; but those who live in accordance with the Spirit have their minds set on what the Spirit desires. The mind of sinful man is death but the mind controlled by the Spirit is life and peace."* (Romans 8:5-6).

I have used spiritual language. Psychologists may prefer to use the jargon of psychology. This transformation from the sinful nature to the spiritual nature is the essence of cognitive therapy. According to Dr. Mark McMinn, *"The goal of cognitive therapy is to help clients break out of their unproductive cycles of thinking and feeling by giving them tools to think in more accurate ways.''xxxiv*

Let it be unmistakably understood that cognitive therapy or any humanly devised therapy cannot change the sinful nature. Such therapy in the hands of a skilled counselor will only serve to bring conscious awareness of the client's dysfunctional condition. To replace the dysfunctional thinking and behaving requires a miracle from God, the miracle of transformation, which can only be effected by the sanctifying work of the Holy Spirit. The sinner who admits his erroneous beliefs and thoughts must now replace them with accurate systems of thinking and responding. This is the function of the Holy Spirit. The counselor's role would be to facilitate the client's understanding of the role of the Holy Spirit and the dynamics of the process of transformation.

Keeping this in mind, let us go back to Brian and Betty. If we allow for Betty's rebuke of Brian could Brian have averted the crisis? If Brian had been daily pursuing the transformation of his mind by allowing the work of the Holy Spirit then he would have been better prepared to deal with his wife's rebuke. Unfortunately he simply responded to his carnal nature, which is the pattern of the world. Had his mind been focused on the spiritual demands of holiness he would have been able to accept the rebuke and calmly explain his position and allow for a healthy discussion.

In other words, he could have chosen to respond in a way that would have resolved the potential crisis. But by reason of habitually thinking and practicing the way of the world he automatically responded in a dysfunctional manner thus precipitating a bigger crisis. Hence the need to practice a lifestyle of responding according to the spirit and not of the flesh.

8: Building Spiritual Muscle

But one may rightly ask, "How is this transformation to be achieved?" Within the answer to this question is the key to holiness and the real answer to all of life's current and potential crises. When properly understood and diligently applied even the worst crisis can be dealt with in a way that is functionally wholesome. The real tragedy in today's rushed world is that people, even Christians, do not really understand the theology of suffering and spiritual warfare. Spiritual warfare is real! Spiritual war is being waged daily.

The Bible informs us very unequivocally that "*our struggle is not against flesh and blood, but against the rulers, against the authorities, against the powers of this dark world and against the spiritual forces of evil in the heavenly realms*" (Eph. 5:12). Therefore, Paul, the writer of Ephesians, advises that Christians should "*be strong in the Lord and in His mighty power*" and that they should "*put on the full armor of God so that you can take your stand against the devil's schemes.*

In the days before high tech war waging a successful war against an enemy nation or tribe depended to a large extent on the physical armor and physical muscle of the fighters. Soldiers were trained to build and condition their muscles for strength, flexibility, speed and endurance. Soldiers with the right equipment and superb muscular conditioning were more likely to survive than those who wore inferior armor and were poorly conditioned. Likewise, in spiritual war the soldier needs to have the right spiritual armor and properly conditioned spiritual muscle to defeat the enemy.

Christians cannot avoid the war. The spiritual battles are built into very fabric of life because of the entrance of sin into the world. Since therefore, we cannot avoid the spiritual war the intelligent course of action would be to prepare ourselves to win the battles and thereby minimize the crisis response. How then can one prepare to win these battles and minimize the dysfunctional responses to crisis events that we cannot avoid?

We need to build our spiritual muscles. And this

requires diligent attention to what is commonly called, "the spiritual disciplines". The spiritual disciplines are foundational to building spiritual muscles that would furnish us with strength, flexibility, speed and endurance. I wish to spend a little time on six absolutely vital disciplines that are guaranteed to build very strong spiritual muscles. They are: worship, fellowship, study, meditation, prayer and fasting. The implementation of these disciplines will not prevent all crisis circumstances. But they will certainly equip you to deal effectively with any crisis condition so that even if your external world is collapsing around you your internal world will remain stable and secure. In other words, the crisis event over which you may have little or no control will not result in a dysfunctional response. Your spiritual muscles, which would have been adequately developed, would automatically respond to offset the negative and keep you whole in Jesus.

Worship

There can be no human activity greater or more important than the worship of God. We were created by God to worship Him. Jesus Christ explained that "*a time is coming and has now come when the true worshippers will worship the Father in spirit and truth, for they are the kind of worshippers the Father seeks. God is spirit and His worshippers must worship in spirit and truth*" (John 4:23-24) No activity can bring one closer to God than to simply worship Him because He is God, holy and worthy to revered. To worship God is to enter into His glory and drink deeply from His presence and radiance. It is to experience the greatest joy that can ever be experienced on the human level. It is the most satisfying, fulfilling, rejuvenating, liberating and wholesome activity that any human can ever attain. Nothing even comes close. How tragic that millions of people have no idea of the beauty, purity and exhilaration that comes from worshipping the Only God of the universe.

Worship can be private (you and God only) or corporate (with other believers). Both types are important for building spiritual muscle. In private or public worship the worshipper enters into the Most Holy Place and communes with God in songs of praise and adoration, prayers of praise and adoration, and thanksgiving. He kneels, sits, prostrates himself on the floor, stands, lifts up his hands, claps his hands, shouts with joy as he feels the glory of the Lord shining down upon Him. During such worship nothing in the world matters but the pure, unadulterated worship of God. The ecstasy and peace that are produced are beyond words of any language.

In authentic worship, the worshipper begins to experience the love, power and holiness of the Omnipotent God who loves him. In turn he desires to respond in a way that loves God with all the heart, soul and mind even as Jesus commands. This worship manifests itself in the totality of the person as he responds physically (the use of his body), emotionally (very deep feelings of joy, delight, ecstasy) and spiritually (a sense of connecting to the very throne of God as the Holy Spirit directs). The worshipper becomes finely attuned to the urgings and promptings of the Holy Spirit. The end result of such worship is transformation. And a transformed person is a spiritually strong person. He is ready for battle.

Fellowship

Fellowship is another corporate discipline that is critical for building strong spiritual muscles. Fellowship is a matter of believers coming together to worship God and spend time sharing, caring, enjoying a meal together, and providing a support system for each other. It is the principle of love in operation so that all believers may be strengthened. God commands, *"let us not give up meeting together as some are in the habit of doing but let us encourage one another — and all the more as you see the Day approaching"* Heb. 10:25). Unfortunately, many in the Christian community have neglected this command to their own spiritual detriment.

As a pastor I have seen first hand the sorry plight of many who left the fellowship of a congregation, did not find another but simply made the decision to become independent

81

Christians. In a short time they had lost their love and passion for God and the holy things of God. Their lives became morally and spiritually bankrupt. Satan moved in as a wolf moves in upon a lone sheep or a lion pounces upon the straying deer and inflicted much damage upon them. I have seen their lives move from crisis to crisis and their lives become broken and battered. They no longer had any spiritual muscle to fight the spiritual battles.

Many who choose to break off fellowship with the corporate body of believers offer weak excuses to justify and rationalize their departure. Granted it is not wrong to leave a fellowship if one is searching for a healthier congregation but to excuse oneself totally from organized fellowship is to give Satan an open invitation to attack you. Oftentimes the excuses are a reflection of their own unwillingness to grow in wholeness and holiness, or a way to continue a lifestyle of secret sin or to get away from Christian responsibilities. No excuse is valid. To fail to fellowship on a regular basis is to cause your spiritual muscles to become flabby and the net result would be a major crisis in your life in order that God may get your attention for you own good. We cannot play games with God for He knows the hearts of all. I am reminded of the independent Christian who defended his position by arguing that the church had too many hypocrites. The pastor who was working with him replied that "the church always has room for one more".

Study & Meditation

It is a sad commentary on Christians in this nation that time is always the excuse for not attending to the vital godly disciplines required for building strong spiritual muscles. Talk to the average person about study of the Holy Bible, meditation (most do not even know what this means), prayer and fasting and the automatic response is that they do not have time. And yet the very people who argue that they do not have time spend numerous hours looking at television or reading books and magazines that sap their spiritual power and set

82

them on the path to major crises.

A few years ago a friend gave me two poems which he had found somewhere. I urge you to honestly consider these poems and judge yourself. The author is unknown. Those who contend that they do not have time for God may find these poems very insightful and penetrating. Use them for some serious soul searching.

The 23ʳᵈ Channel

The TV is my shepherd, I shall not want
It makes me lie down on the sofa
It leads me away from the faith
It destroys my soul
It leads me in the path of sex and violence for the sponsor's sake
Yea, though I walk in the shadow of Christian responsibilities
There will be no interruption, for the TV is with me
Its cable and remote control, they comfort me
It prepares a commercial for me in the presence of my worldliness
It anoints my head with humanism and consumerism
My coveting runneth over
Surely, laziness and ignorance shall follow me all the days of my life
And I shall dwell in the house watching TV forever
(Author unknown)

The Holy Bible & The TV Guide

On the table side by side;
The Holy Bible and the TV guide
One's well worn but cherished with pride;
Not the Bible but the TV guide
One's used daily to help folk decide;
Not the Bible, it's the TV guide

As pages are turned, what will they see?
Oh, what does it matter, turn on the TV
Then confusion reigns, they can't all agree;
On what they will watch on the old TV
So they open the book in which they confide;
Not the Bible, it's the TV guide
The Word of God is seldom read;
Maybe a verse e'er they fall into bed
Exhausted and sleepy and tired as can be;
Not from reading the Bible, but from watching TV
So then back to the table, side by side,
Are the Holy Bible and the TV guide.
No time for prayer, no time for the Word.
The way of salvation is seldom heard.
Abiding in Christ so full and free,
Is found in the Bible, not on TV.
(Author unknown)

If we feed on a diet of unhealthful foods our bodies will become highly susceptible to diseases. Similarly if we "nourish" our mind and spirit with the culture of darkness then we will become spiritually weak and easily susceptible to emotional and spiritual afflictions. We would be rendered ill equipped to wage effective war against Satan when he strikes. Therefore it is imperative that soldiers of Jesus Christ study and meditate upon the Word of God on a regular basis.

Jesus Christ made it abundantly clear that the truth will set us free. "You will know the truth and the truth will set you free" **(John 8:32)**. Where can we find the truth? The Word of God is truth. The study of God's word brings authentic enlightenment and frees us from bondage to fears, anxieties, worries and other debilitating emotional baggage. God's Word removes the fog of deception that blinds millions and keeps them enslaved to a life of crisis. The person who spends hours reading secular materials will be negatively affected. He will become a victim of the darkness prevalent in today's decadent culture. The only antidote for such darkness is to come into the light which is found in the Holy Bible.

The apostle, Paul, admonished Timothy to study the Scriptures. How else would Timothy be able to discern the good from the evil? How can any Christian distinguish the authentic from the counterfeit? Will you trust your limited human experience and understanding? The obvious answer is to diligently study the Holy Bible so that we may know the mind of God and become transformed. Paul reminds us that, *"all Scripture is God-breathed and is useful for teaching, rebuking, correcting and training in righteousness, so that the man of God may be thoroughly equipped for every good work"* **(II Tim. 3:16-17)**. There can be no compromise on this matter. Only the Holy Bible can adequately prepare us to live as ambassadors for Christ. The Holy Bible is God's manual to us for living the abundant life. Those who prefer to spend more time with secular materials are unwittingly weakening their defenses against Satan and sin and diminishing their effectiveness as servants of God.

The study of the Holy Bible and meditation often go well together. This is why I have chosen to place these two under one heading even though they are two separate disciplines designed to build powerful spiritual muscles. Whereas study is an intellectual and analytical exercise designed to widen one's knowledge and bring one into truth meditation is devotional and contemplative. Meditation serves to deepen our understanding of God's word, internalize His will and then obey Him.

Of course, the normal reaction to the word meditation is the one associated with the Eastern religions as practiced in India. In this type of meditation no real transformation takes place. The devotee simply empties his mind of the worldly things but never finds God. He becomes detached from the material existence but never attached to the God of the Universe. For the Christian meditation is the art of seeking to understand and internalize the will of God for his life so that he may become deeply attached to God and experience authentic transformation. It is about filling the mind with Jesus Christ, pursuing intimacy with God and surrendering oneself to whatever God desires.

The great servant of God, David, understood the depths and purposes of meditation. From him we can learn much as we study the Psalms. In **Psalm 119:97-104** we find these powerful words that can serve as a guide for our meditation.

"Oh, how I love your law!
I meditate on it all day long
Your commands make me wiser than my enemies
For they are ever with me.
I have more insight than all my teachers
For I meditate on your statutes.
I have more understanding than the elders,
For I obey your precepts.
I have kept my feet from every evil path
So that I might obey your word.
I have not departed from your laws
For you yourself have taught me.
How sweet are your words to my taste
Sweeter than honey to my mouth
I gain understanding from your precepts
Therefore I hate every wrong path"

It should be very obvious that while study and meditation are two different disciplines they work together to effect transformation in the person. This transformation serves to equip the servant of God to fight the good fight and not become a victim of disequilibrium. The spiritual muscles are better conditioned to face any crisis and remain stable and secure.

Prayer & Fasting

While study and meditation furnish the soldier with a solid, steady and immovable base from which to fight yet more is needed. The spiritual muscles need strength and endurance. The successful soldier must have an indomitable spirit, an unwavering dedication, and an unflinching commitment. This is where prayer and fasting become absolutely essential in establishing an impenetrable defense system to withstand any attacks of Satan and society. It is by prayer and fasting that we can be equipped to minimize the dysfunctional response to the inevitable crises in life. It is fatally unfortunate that we humans are so busy in trying to secure a comfortable living that we ignore the need to live a life dedicated to the God-ordained purpose for our existence. Consequently, people do not set aside quality time to build a quality relationship with the very God who desires to be at the heart of their being. It is prayer and fasting that lifts us from the earth bound perspective to the eternal perspective, which enables us to become functionally whole. The majority of mankind live with the earthy perspective. Those who are earth bound cannot scale the heavenly heights. To wage war against heavenly forces require that we move out of this earth bound dimension and reach to the heavens. Prayer and fasting (along with worship) help us to live and experience the divine realm.

Perhaps, some may be thinking that I have entered into some type of esoteric state by using such terminology as in the above paragraph. To assuage your fears consider what Paul says in his letter to the church at Ephesus. *"And God raised us up with Christ and seated us with Him in the heavenly realms in Christ Jesus"* (Eph. 2:6). To the church at Colosse Paul wrote, *"Since then you have been raised with Christ, set your hearts on things above, where Christ is seated at the right hand of God. Set your minds on things above, not on earthly things. For you died and your life is now hidden with Christ in God"* (Col. 3:1-3).

Most people are too focused on the things that satisfy the flesh to even consider a fast. In an age of an abundance of food available at every turn on every street why should anybody want to go without food and drink for a day or more? The painful truth is that humans are too focused on the satiation of the physical senses. We become enslaved to food, fun and pleasure. Fasting can correct such enslavement and place us on the divine platform to become all that God wants us to be. With fasting we come to see our humanity in all its weaknesses and become more dependent upon God for our strength. And that is exactly what God desires that we see and live; to learn to fully trust Him for all our needs.

Assuming that you fast according to the biblical model there are several benefits to be derived. I will address the spiritual benefits. It is also evident that there are physical benefits. By Biblical model I mean that fasting must not be done in a legalistic or ritualistic way as a means of scoring points with God for salvation. It is simply the humbling of oneself before God to seek His will and purpose and learn to become totally dependent upon Him for our sustenance. Fasting must never be an effort to impose our will upon God. It is not for us to direct God. We seek His direction. If you are looking for some Scriptural guidelines for true fasting I recommend that you study Isaiah 58:1-14.

Keeping in mind that fasting and prayer must go together here are a few definite spiritual benefits of fasting:

The denial of physical foods helps us to learn the discipline of the emotional and spiritual. Self-control becomes easier when fasting is done on a regular basis.

Fasting may bring to light any physical addictions, emotional addictions or spiritual weaknesses within us. God will reveal to us the things that control us.

Fasting teaches us humility. As we experience hunger and our physical energy and physical strength diminish we become far more aware of how weak the flesh really is. Consequently we will learn to glory in the things of God and not the things of the flesh.

We begin to appreciate the plan of God for people in general. Our perspective about life changes and we become more balanced in everything.

We drink in deeply of God's power and so are far better equipped to wage the spiritual war against Satan, sin and the culture of darkness and thus live more fully in wholeness and holiness.

Specifically on the matter of prayer, Richard Foster

shares some very insightful thoughts. He writes, *"the heart of God is an open wound of love. He aches over our distance and preoccupation. He mourns that we do not draw near to Him. He grieves that we have forgotten Him. He weeps over our obsession with muchness and manyness. He longs for our presence."xxxv* How tragic that Satan has placed numerous distractions in our way so as to cause us to travel the road to crisis while we are left powerless to respond to the crisis in a spiritually beneficial way. As Foster further elaborates, *"For too long we have been in a far country; a country of noise and hurry and crowds, a country of climb and push and shove, a country of frustration and fear and intimidation. And he welcomes us home: home to serenity and peace and joy, home to friendship and fellowship and openness, home to intimacy and acceptance and affirmation."xxxvi*

Jesus taught mankind the value and the method of prayer by his teachings and lifestyle. But most people are too busy to listen to the voice of God, whether through His words as spoken by Jesus or through quiet times of fasting and solitude. In fact, it is the deliberate plan of Satan to keep people busy with the mundane dimensions of life so that they would stay far from God and the real important dimensions of life.

If Satan can keep people away from listening to the voice of God then they would naturally live lifestyles that lead to crisis and respond to such self-created crises in sinful and dysfunctional ways. Not surprisingly thousands who claim to be Christians are faithless and powerless against Satan and his wiles. They have failed to fortify themselves to wage battle against the spiritual forces of darkness and become putty in the hands of the evil one as he hurls his darts of discouragement and arrows of fire against unsuspecting and ill-equipped humans.

Tragically, many even begin to doubt the love and power of the God who desires to help them walk through the valley of the shadow of death. What a clever counterfeit Satan has foisted upon a highly materialistic, individualistic and hedonistic society. The most painful part of this is that such a dysfunctional lifestyle is avoidable if only humanity returns to the true God with prayer and fasting.

By prayer and fasting we enter into personal and private dialogue with God. We deliberately invite Him to come to us and reveal Himself and His will so that we may begin to see His purpose in our lives. As we begin to actually enjoy His companionship in a very real way we are motivated to spend more time with Him and less time with the secular. We learn the method of relinquishment of our desires and will and gladly accept His will and guidance in our lifestyle. As our eyes and mind become increasingly aware of His power and holiness and love for us we find it easier to surrender our will completely to His sovereign goodness thus facilitating the life of Jesus in us. Like the Apostle Paul, we too can then say, that *"it is no longer I who live, but it is Christ who lives in me. And the life I now live in the flesh I live by faith in the Son of God, who loved me and gave Himself for me"* (Gal. 2:19-20).

This awareness of Jesus living in us sharpens our senses to the dynamics of the particular crisis so that we are attuned to the will of God and are thus empowered to actually become thankful for the crisis. Thus by prayer and fasting we are enabled to change our perspective on the circumstances of the crisis even while we are unable to change the circumstances. So it is evident that prayer and fasting can serve to minimize the disequilibrium created by a crisis because by understanding and experiencing the mind of Jesus, the presence of God and the empowerment of the Holy Spirit we are prepared and capable of walking through the difficult times without making the crisis even greater.

9: Depression

I wish to deal with one of the most common dysfunctional responses to crisis events. I will examine the subject of depression. I am aware that depression can also be treated as a crisis event but for the most part it is a response to other crises. Let me reiterate that the matter here is the minimization of the negative response to the crisis event. So the assumption is that the person is already experiencing the crisis event. For example, the person may have already contracted a deadly disease, lost a spouse through divorce or death, suffered severe financial losses, or facing the tragic consequences of a relationship fallout or the loss of a prized possession. Thus the issue is not the reversal of the event but more importantly, the response to the fact of the currently existing crisis event.

I have deliberately chosen the problem of depression because the statistics indicate that depression is the most widespread response to crises, medical, social, emotional, or spiritual. In fact, depression has often been called the "common cold" of psychological problems. It is reported that nine million adults in the United States are victims of depression every year. When we consider that this figure accounts only for those reported then we could perceive that the problem is much bigger. There are millions of people, particularly, religious types, who suffer silently through depression for fear that others would know they have such a "horrible" affliction. So it would not be far fetched to estimate that in any given year there may be as many as twenty million people suffering with depression. Consider also that about fifty thousand of these would choose the ultimate dysfunctional response by committing suicide. With such alarming statistics I think it is imperative that I devote serious attention to this subject of depression.

Since this book is not specifically a study on depression I will not deal with every aspect of depression. My purpose is to make the point that the pursuit of wholeness and holiness as a lifestyle will significantly minimize the dysfunctional response of depression. It must, of course, be understood that in many cases depression is endogenous. In such cases, depression is the event and not the chosen response. In such cases of depression the individual is manifesting the symptoms of depression because there is a biochemical deficiency within the body. In these cases the victim does not have much control. But even then, the active presence of the Holy Spirit in his life can minimize the level of dysfunction. My concern is primarily reactive depression because this type is, by far, the most common type of depression.

It is necessary to examine the typical symptoms of depression before making the case for the minimization of the dysfunctional response. According to the Diagnostic and Statistical Manual of Mental Disorders five or more of the following symptoms must be present during the same two week period and represent a change from previous functioning in order that it be classified as a major Depressive Episode.

> Depressed mood most of the day, nearly every day.
> Markedly diminished interest or pleasure in all,
> or almost all activities most of the day,
> nearly every day.
> Significant weight loss when not dieting or
> weight gain, or decrease or increase in appetite
> nearly every day.
> Insomnia or hypersomnia nearly every day.
> Psychomotor agitation or retardation nearly
> every day.
> Fatigue or loss of energy nearly every day.
> Feelings of worthlessness or excessive or
> inappropriate guilt nearly every day.
> Diminished ability to think or concentrate, or
> indecisiveness, nearly every day.
> Recurrent thoughts of death, recurrent
> suicidal ideation without a specific plan or
> a suicide attempt or a specific plan for
> committing suicide.[xxxvii]

The fact that millions of people, including Christians, experience these symptoms as a way of life is evidence of the destructive work of Satan whose main goal is to destroy humanity's relationship with God and thus forfeit life eternal. Can the pursuit of wholeness and holiness minimize these dysfunctional responses? Absolutely! I am not suggesting that holiness will eliminate all depression and make a Christian immune to depression. Even great men of faith, like Elijah, suffered bouts of depression. My point is that much of the misery of depression can be significantly diminished in regard to duration and intensity.

Indeed, the very response of depression may serve to make a person much more spiritually powerful and useful to God for serving humanity. In other words, depression, if properly understood and processed, may serve to make a person more functionally whole and become a greater vessel for God's calling upon a person's life. Thus, a crisis event which precipitated a dysfunctional response can be turned into a positive experience and be of benefit for thousands of others.

When we closely examine the symptoms of depression we see that the core problem is hopelessness. The depressed person enters a period of intense darkness through which the person views all aspects of life. His view is not consistent with truth and reality but is a cognitive distortion that renders the victim hopeless. This is where the trained helper can be of tremendous assistance in redirecting the person's thinking to see through the darkness. In the pursuit of holiness the person will come to understand that the hopelessness is the product of Satan's deception to lead him away from his relationship with God. Often, depressed people have lost their connection with Jesus Christ and the Holy Spirit. They see life only through the lens of depression. The despair, darkness and loss of joy only serve to exacerbate the feelings of hopelessness.

The depressed person needs to internalize the fact of God's never-failing love and readiness to bring him out of this period of depression. It is not an easy transition but if the person had already been pursuing holiness the job of the helper is much easier. If on the other hand, the person had never pursued holiness the counselor faces a very herculean task to bring this depressed human into the light. Hence the reason for Christians to make holiness a daily way of life so that when crisis events arise and depression follows as a natural consequence they could draw upon the spiritual resources which they have already developed through years of practice and successful implementation.

It is imperative for the Christian to know and believe that God has promised to be with us always. He has said that He would not abandon us nor forsake us. God cannot lie; His word is truth and therefore we can be assured of His promises. By pursuing the culture of holiness through the spiritual disciplines we are able to internalize His faithfulness and maintain our faith when the storms of life crash upon us and the circumstances seem beyond our control. It is when we can no longer be in control that He has to step in and take control. And that is the substance of faith; to actually believe in the reality of the things we cannot see with our physical eyes but which have been guaranteed by God. With the physical senses we feel hopeless but with the spiritual senses we know that God promises to bring deliverance in spite of the darkness that surrounds us. So, I repeat, depression is not the inevitable response. For those who have not tasted of this liberating truth depression may become a way of life until death. The Christian must never lose sight of the truth that "when I cannot cope Jesus offers hope."

10: Alcohol Abuse & Alcoholism

This section on alcohol abuse could be equally appropriate in the chapter on "Minimizing the Crisis Event" but, like depression, I have chosen to place it here because the abuse of alcohol is often a response to crisis events. Surely, alcohol abuse is also a crisis event that is one hundred percent preventable. But it is equally true, perhaps even more correct to view the abuse of alcohol as a dysfunctional response to other problems in a person's life, particularly emotional crises.

Another point of clarification is that alcohol abuse and alcoholism are not exactly the same thing. Since this book is not on Alcohol-Induced Disorders but rather on minimizing crisis and maximizing one's life for God, I do not consider it pertinent to deal with the distinctions between alcoholism and alcohol abuse. Suffice it to say that alcoholism is perceived by the medical experts as a disease often termed, "alcohol dependence syndrome."

Alcohol abuse differs from alcoholism in that it does not involve a strong physiological craving for alcohol or a physical dependence on the substance. It is believed by some in the medical and psychological field that alcoholism can be inherited. Alcohol abuse, however, is primarily the response to one's social and emotional environment. My primary concern is that alcohol abuse with all of its horrible consequences in terms of deadly diseases, fractured families, aborted babies or permanently damaged babies, emotional traumas, automobile accidents, industrial accidents, job losses, financial waste, homicides and suicides can be prevented.

According to The National Institute on Alcohol Abuse and Alcoholism (NIAAA), 14 million Americans, currently, abuse alcohol or are alcoholic. There is evidence to believe that several millions more adults engage in risky drinking patterns that could lead to alcohol problems. Additionally, 53 percent of adults in America report that one or more of their close relatives have a drinking problem. What does this mean in real human terms? The NIAAA informs us that, *"heavy drinking can increase the risk for certain cancers, especially* *those of the liver, esophagus, throat, and larynx. It can also cause liver cirrhosis, immune system problems, brain damage, and harm to the fetus during pregnancy. In addition, drinking increases the risk of death from automobile crashes, recreational accidents, and on-the-job accidents and also increases the likelihood of homicide and suicide. In purely economic terms, alcohol-use problems cost society approximately $100 billion per year. In human terms, the costs are incalculable. "xxxviii*

Further statistical information provided by the National Council on Alcoholism and Drug Dependence (NCADD) reveals clearly the monstrous crisis of alcohol abuse. It is very sobering and frightening to examine the magnitude of the alcohol problem. I consider it germane to the heart of my lifestyle model of wholeness and holiness to present some of these grim statistics.

Alcohol is the most widely used psychoactive drug in the USA.

Alcohol contributes to 100,000 deaths annually, making it the third leading cause of preventable mortality in the US, after tobacco and diet/activity patterns.

In 1992, more than seven percent of the population ages 18 years and older – nearly 13.8 million Americans – had problems with drinking, including 8.1 million people who are alcoholic. Almost three times as many men (9.8m) as women (3.9m) were problem drinkers, and prevalence was highest for both sexes in the 18 to 29 years old age group.

About 43% of US adults, 76 million people, have been exposed to alcoholism in the family: they grew up with or married an alcoholic or a problem drinker or had a blood relative who was ever an alcoholic or problem drinker. An estimated 6.6 million children under the age of 18 years live in households with at least one alcoholic parent.

64% of high school seniors report that they have been drunk; more than 31% say that they have had five or more drinks in a row during the last two weeks.

People who begin drinking before the age of 15 are

four times more likely to develop alcoholism than those who begin at age 21.

From 1985 to 1992, the economic costs of alcoholism and alcohol-related problems rose 42% to $148 billion. Two thirds of the costs related to lost productivity, either due to alcohol-related illness (45.7%) or premature death (21.2%). On average, untreated alcoholics incur general health care costs at least 100% higher than those of nonalcoholics.

Based on victim reports, each year 183,000 rapes and sexual assaults involve alcohol by use of the offender, as do just over 197,000 robberies, about 661,000 aggravated assaults and nearly 1.7 million simple assaults.

Fetal alcohol syndrome (FAS), which can occur when women drink during pregnancy, is the leading known environmental cause of mental retardation in the Western world. Each year about 12,000 babies are born with the physical signs and intellectual disabilities associated with FAS, and thousands more experience the somewhat lesser disabilities of fetal alcohol effects.

Studies of suicide victims in the general population show that about 20% of such suicide victims are alcoholic.

41% of all traffic fatalities (the leading cause of accidental death) are alcohol-related; alcoholics are nearly five times more likely than others to die in motor vehicle crashes.

Estimates suggest that alcohol is associated with between 47% and 65% of adult drownings.

Up to 40% of industrial fatalities and 47% of industrial injuries can be linked to alcohol consumption and alcoholism.

If ever there was a case to prevent alcohol abuse the above quoted information is enough to win a conviction. And there is a lot more information available supporting the fact that crises caused by alcohol are totally preventable. Dr. Charles Henneken, an endowed professor of medicine at Harvard Medical School says, *"the difference between drinking small or large amounts is the difference between preventing and causing premature death."* [xxxix]

According to the same article, the scientists involved in the study of alcohol warn people about the dangerous aspects of excessive drinking: *"increased accidents, liver damage and the severe psychosocial toll on the individual, the family and society. Fifty percent of fatal car accidents involve drunk drivers."*[xl] Numerous research studies support the conclusion that the abuse of alcohol is a preventable crisis. And yet, alcohol continues to remain a staple item in the lifestyles of millions of Americans and, indeed, hundreds of millions of people across this earth.

The lamentable fact is that in spite of every government and community program the abuse of alcohol continues. College students seek to fill the unmet emotional needs and the spiritual void in their lives by the indulgence of alcohol. Frustrated spouses seek to find peace in the midst of a shattered relationship by drowning their pain and loneliness in bars and pubs. And the restless and insecure people of the world seek solace and escape from the reality of their troubled existence by filling themselves with alcohol. Why?

The heart of the problem is spiritual. In one sense the solution is so simple that one wonders why it is not implemented. If only people were taught from childhood the value of pursuing wholeness and holiness and the institutions of society were structured to reinforce the pursuit of holiness millions of crises would come to and end and billions of dollars could be channeled into more productive sectors of society.

The institutions of our culture, which have the financial resources and the political clout to make a difference, remain powerless in the advance of this Goliath, the abuse of alcohol. The reason is obvious. A spiritual problem cannot be resolved by physical or medical or psychological methods. A spiritual problem demands a spiritual solution.

The horrific tragedy of crisis wreaked by alcohol is symptomatic of a culture that has forsaken God and His laws of holiness. The Holy Bible has clearly forbidden the misuse of alcohol. In fact, drunkenness is sin and those who practice such cannot enter the kingdom of God. Yet alcohol is glorified and eulogized in this culture of crisis and death. Television, magazines, and other mass media often associate alcohol with success and power and style and status.

In a society where people are searching for meaning and purpose the internal void designed by God to be filled by the Holy Spirit is often "filled" by a counterfeit that leads to hell. Alcohol cannot fill the void, which God intended to be filled in another way. Deep spiritual yearnings were deliberately created by God so that people will respond to His call upon their lives.

Counselors, pastors and all Christian helpers across America need to become filled with Jesus Christ in their own lives and then they will be able to equip others so that together we can halt this growing nightmare that has become a colossal waste of time, money and life.

If you are facing a crisis because of alcohol abuse you need to confess it before God and seek His divine help urgently before this addiction destroys you and your family. Heed the voice of God and be filled with Him.

For at least six thousand years of biblical history mankind has rebelled against the holiness of God. He has, unwittingly, facilitated the rule of Satan. The result is that people practice a lifestyle that leads to crises and dysfunctional responses to such crises.

In short he has allowed sin to reign. God, in His abundant mercy and grace decided to heal the breach between man and Himself and so became incarnate and paid the price for the sins of the world.

In return, God commanded that mankind should accept the sacrifice of Jesus and thus experience freedom from the heartaches and emptiness of sinful living. But alas, mankind persists in his unbelief and so the lifestyle of crisis continues as millions pay the price daily.

Jesus, when he entered the city of Jerusalem lamented, *"O Jerusalem, Jerusalem, you who kill the prophets and stone those sent to you, how often I have longed to gather your children together, as a hen gathers her chicks under her wings, but you were not willing."* (Matthew 23:37).

Alcohol continues to destroy, maim, wreak havoc, demolish families, and cause premature suffering and death as people seek the temporary relief of stress and the momentary pleasures of sin.

11: Victory by Faith

The millions of people who have committed suicide over the years as a result of any specific reason or combination of reasons could have averted such a tragic response if only they had known how to avail themselves of the power of the God of the Universe. It is true that there are times in the lives of all people, Christian or not, when the enormity of the negative circumstances rage as an overwhelming flood ready to destroy everything in its path. But it is also true that the same God who permits the floods of despair and depression has the power to create a path through the sea of depression.

I can use the wonderful illustration of Peter as recorded in Scripture. The writer, Matthew, records an incident in which Peter asked the Lord for permission to walk on the water on which Jesus was walking. Jesus invited Peter to meet him on the water and Peter quickly responded. Note what happened as told by Matthew, *"Then Peter got down out of the boat, walked on the water and came toward Jesus. But when he saw the wind, he was afraid and beginning to sink, cried out, 'Lord, save me!' Immediately Jesus reached out his hand and caught him. 'You of little faith,' he said, 'why did you doubt?"* (Matthew 14:29-31).

This incident typifies the weakness of human flesh in the face of circumstances outside of our immediate control. For a little while, Peter did actually walk on the water. In effect, Peter was performing a miraculous feat until he took his eyes off Jesus and refocused on the earthly circumstances. The physical fact of the raging wind upon the waters impressed upon his mind that walking on the water was an impossibility. He doubted the presence and power of Jesus not because Jesus was incapable but rather because of the threatening reality of that which his limited human experience understood. And in that moment he found himself sinking into the water.

Jesus taught Peter a very powerful spiritual lesson, one that he would, no doubt, have remembered often in his work as an apostle after the death and resurrection of Jesus. The pursuit of holiness demands that we never lose sight of the power, love and availability of God in all circumstances no matter how impossible a situation may appear. The person who is assured of the continuous presence of God in his life possess a wonderful advantage over others in dealing with any crisis event that life presents, whether by his fault or the fault of another. The very assurance of divine power facilitates a functional response to the crisis event.

The tragedy is that most people do not really understand faith as defined by God. Faith is not about what you feel. Too many Christians confuse faith with feelings. Feelings are just that, feelings. And feelings are essentially emotions generated by internal and external stimuli which impact upon the thinking process. In actuality, feelings are the natural product of being flesh and blood. This is not to imply that feelings are inherently wrong. By no means! God is the One who gave us the wonderful capacity to experience feelings. But faith based on feelings is not biblical faith. Authentic faith simply believes that God is exactly what He says He is and that He will do exactly what He promises to do.

In the famous "faith chapter" of the Holy Bible we are given unequivocal instructions regarding the matter of faith. God speaks to us and informs us that *"without faith it is impossible to please God, because anyone who comes to Him must believe that He exists and that He rewards those who diligently seek Him"* **(Heb. 11:6).** We cannot have the victorious life without faith in who and what God is. God is everything He claims to be. By His word as recorded in the Holy Bible, He is omnipotent, omniscient, omnipresent, faithful, compassionate, merciful, unchanging, personal and love. The problem is most people do not really believe in their hearts that God is everything that He claims to be. Unless we believe God for what He is we cannot have the full blessings He desires to give us.

It is a fact of life that what we believe about life will determine how we live. If for example a person believes (as many do) that money is the most important thing in life then such a person will make all decisions in the context of that belief. In the same way what we believe about God determines the nature and quality of our relationship with God. What we need to internalize is that our beliefs about God do not change who and what God is. God is exactly what He is as revealed in Scripture. To not believe Him for what He says does not change Him but it does affect us in what we will be able to accomplish in life. If we limit God's power and influence then our lives cannot attain to the highest level possible. Hence we must believe that He is all that He says and believe that He does reward those who diligently seek Him.

So we see that faith is not based on feelings. Neither is faith based on human logic or intellectual reasoning. Human logic is human logic. Intellectual reasoning is intellectual reasoning. Faith cannot be dependent upon human logic or intellectual reasoning. Faith is not subject to the laws that govern the natural processes of life. Faith is supernatural, rooted in the power and holiness of God who is above His creation and not subject to His creation. When the Red Sea opened to make a way for the Israelites to escape the pursuing Egyptians God was demonstrating His power over His creation. To the Israelites the situation seemed hopeless but God had already planned to use this crisis event to teach a powerful lesson in faith. The parting of the Red Sea defied the typical logic and reason of human beings. By human logic there was no way out of this crisis for them. From the human perspective the only options were to face the Egyptians and fight or surrender. But God has far more options. His options are not limited by human intelligence or by anything in the Universe. God is bigger than the biggest crisis anybody can ever face.

The reason that most people live with defeat and actually accept the culture of crisis as normative is because they fail to grasp the power and love of God. In any given crisis, the tendency is to focus on our own inadequacies and incapacity. It is certainly necessary to admit one's own inadequacy but the focus must not remain at that level. The recognition of one's own incapacity to deal effectively with a particular crisis or problem should serve as a springboard to lift our focus above the earthly level on to the divine level. In so doing we will then see the God who is able, capable and available if only we would trust His power and love to get us out of the seemingly hopeless situation.

Victory over the challenges and difficulties of this life is not obtained by the use of our own limited resources. We must avail ourselves of the limitless resources of the God who has promised deliverance. When we focus on His strength, His power, His unlimited capacity and His love for us then faith replaces doubt and fear. When faith becomes the operating principle of our lives then the outcome of the battle is no longer dependent upon our puny efforts but on God's unsurpassable strength.

When God called upon Moses to become the leader to deliver the Israelites out of bondage to the Egyptians Moses sought to make every possible excuse to avoid such an assignment. He identified to God his own incapacity for such a huge task. He even complained that he did not possess the eloquence of speech to stand before Pharaoh. But God reminded Moses that He had all power to do whatever was necessary. He assured Moses that, "I will be with you". And God was faithful to His word even though for a little while it seemed that the plight of the Israelites became worse. In fact, even the Israelites complained that Moses had only served to intensify the crisis and bring them more suffering. But God encouraged Moses to stay faithful to the calling. Victory by faith in God and God's promises is assured for all those who do not lose sight of the goal.

The devil will use every method to keep us in a crisis condition. His common methods of warfare are the tools of discouragement, despair, doubt and depression. All of these d's are the tools of his trade. They are the enemies of faith. Only when these d's are removed out of the way can the Christian experience the victory that God desires to make available.

The daily pursuit of wholeness and holiness keeps us constantly focused on the power, holiness and love of God by which our faith will increase. With authentic faith, we have access to the victory over all circumstances because of the power of Christ in us. The Christian is connected to the most powerful force in the universe. The indwelling presence of the Holy Spirit is the guarantor of victory over any crisis, even if the negative circumstances never change.

The apostle, Paul, encourages Christians in Romans 8:35-39 by writing, *"Who shall separate us from the love of Christ? Shall trouble or hardship or persecution or famine or nakedness or danger or sword? No, in all these things we are more than conquerors through him who loved us. For I am convinced that neither death nor life, neither angels nor demons, neither the present nor the future, nor any powers, neither height nor depth, nor anything else in all creation, will be able to separate us from the love of God that is in Christ Jesus our Lord."* But this victory is only available to the extent that Christians really believe it and approach God's throne to make request for it. Sadly, many Christians do not really know or exercise their rights and responsibilities as children of The Great God.

12: The Functional Perspective on Crisis

In this section I hope to prove to you that the functional perspective to crisis is the most important dimension in dealing with a crisis. In fact, when this perspective is properly understood the individual actually becomes thankful for the crisis event.

It is my position that Christians need to understand that every crisis event has positive potential for the one experiencing the crisis and, perhaps, serves the divine purposes of God, for this person and those lives who may be touched by the one suffering the crisis. It must never be forgotten that God is sovereign and always in control of the Universe. This God is bigger than any crisis and therefore desires to use every crisis for good in His children. Further, God has a divine purpose for all whom He is calling into a relationship with Him through Jesus Christ. Christians can rest securely in the hands of God because, *"we know that in all things God works for the good of those who love him, who have been called according to his purpose."* (Rom.8:28)

Let me put the subject of crisis in historical perspective. Humanity was ushered into crisis when the very first humans rebelled against the Maker of the Universe. When Adam and Eve sinned, little could they have realized that their sin would create the biggest crisis for all mankind. For in sinning, they incurred the penalty of death for themselves and for all humans thereafter.

The Bible says, *"...sin entered the world through one man, and death through sin, and in this way death came to all men, because all sinned..."* Romans 5:12 (NIV). So sin separated man from God. In fact, according the historical account in Genesis, God banished man from the Garden of Eden. Gen. 3:23 records it as, *"So the Lord God banished him from the Garden of Eden to work the ground from which he had been taken."*

It is even more critical to note that God actually pronounced curses upon Adam and Eve as a result of their act of disobedience. Therefore, mankind is separated from God by sin and thus the whole creation groans until the day of redemption when all things will be made new and there will be no more pain and suffering and death.

But God did not abandon mankind. He determined to rescue humanity by the incarnation of Himself as Jesus Christ, and become the sacrificial lamb for the remission of humanity's sins and so reconcile mankind to God. By this sacrifice eternal life became available as a gift to all who would respond to His divine grace. However, the promise of life eternal did not remove the need for suffering in the flesh. Jesus Christ, himself suffered even though he was without sin. And he assured his followers that they would have to endure trials and tribulations in this physical life. In other words, God has not ever promised a life free from crisis. It is only when a person understands the theology of crisis that he would be equipped to perceive crisis in a functional way and by so doing facilitate the divine purposes intended.

Let me illustrate by use of a case study that began in the latter half of 1998. Sophia is a Christian who desires above all else to live the lifestyle of a Christian. She has three daughters living with her, the eldest being 16 and the youngest is 7. Her husband is not a Christian. Apart from the normal daily stresses of life Sophia lives a fairly comfortable life attending to the daily rigors of life in a big city. She faithfully fellowships with her Christian brothers and sisters and tries to serve her husband and family to the best of her limited ability.

One day Sophia suddenly becomes ill, is rushed to the doctor who advises that she go to the hospital. By the next day, Sophia is rushed into the Intensive Care Unit of the hospital and is kept alive only by the use of modern technology, a respirator and several tubes inserted into her lungs and other parts of the body. This is a major crisis! The husband is shocked, the children are bewildered and the church members are in disbelief! Her mother finds out about her suffering and hastens to the hospital and upon seeing the condition of her daughter she is overwhelmed emotionally. She collapses and must take medication to stay sane. This crisis has now reached major dimensions.

In the meantime, Sophia is struggling to stay alive. Her lungs have collapsed and the doctors are not sure that she will live. The mother, in particular is distraught. Having already suffered the loss of one daughter several years ago, she dreads the outcome of this crisis. The days roll into weeks. Sophia remains in the intensive care and the family is advised by the doctors to be prepared to accept her death. Hundreds of prayers ascend to the throne room of heaven for the healing of Sophia but it seems of no avail. Why such a crisis for a family, more specifically, a young mother who is a Christian? Everybody is baffled, even the doctors who find it abnormal for a woman so young to experience such a health crisis.

The mother, Evelyn, calls the pastor of the church and informs him that she thinks that her daughter is suffering because God needs to get Evelyn's attention. She admits that many years ago she had made a promise to serve God but within the last few years had forsaken the holiness of Jesus Christ and was actually living in a condition of sin. She is convinced that God wants her to return to the faith and the holiness of the Christian life. So she makes the right decision to leave her life of sin and return to God and give God thanks for His goodness. In the meantime, her daughter begins to show signs of recovery. After a few days, Sophia, is released from the hospital and sent home for full recovery. Slowly and painfully gets back to normal but with a few differences.

Evelyn recommits her life to God. But more importantly, Sophia's husband, Bill begins to examine his life especially in the spiritual context. Conflicts continue to occur within the marriage as they struggle through an enormous amount of emotional baggage. The crisis is taking its toll upon them emotionally, relationally and spiritually. But God is working out a fascinating plan. After a few months the husband desires to see the pastor and seeks to know more about Jesus and Christianity. In a few weeks he requests counsel for baptism. He has come to believe in the true God as represented by Jesus Christ. He accepts Jesus as his personal Savior and Lord and becomes a Christian. As I write both husband and wife and the children are actively involved in the life of the congregation and are looking at ways to make an impact for Jesus in their community. How marvelous are the ways of God!

Could Sophia have prevented this medical crisis? Probably. No one can be sure. Could God have prevented the crisis to Sophia? The answer is rather obvious. Of course, God can do as He pleases. He is Sovereign. In retrospect we can see that God's purpose was being worked out. Divine providence was being shaped. A crisis, that for many, was indeed a crisis, was being used by God for a much higher and eternal purpose. God desired to get Bill's attention so that he could be brought to salvation. He also wanted to remind Evelyn of His love for her and of her need to restore her relationship with Him. In His mercy, He allowed Sophia to be suddenly afflicted with a long and severe enough illness to get Bill's attention and bring him to the place of reconciliation so that he could enter into a holy covenant with the Eternal God for his own good.

When we examine the nature and circumstances of this true-life story (the names have been changed) it is understandable that the crisis is major financially, medically and emotionally. How could a loving God permit such a terrible affliction upon one of His own children? From the human perspective it seems senseless and can be terribly devastating in several ways. But God who is omnipotent, omniscient and omnipresent had determined that this crisis event would finally lead to functional wholeness, if only, in the spiritual dimension, in the life of a precious child of His. What people need to understand is that God would do whatever He deems appropriate so that His ultimate purpose for a person or nation is accomplished. And often, that includes crisis conditions and crisis responses. God is concerned with the end result, holiness and eternal salvation.

The apostle, Paul, captures the essence of this dimension of God's sovereignty in Romans 11:33-36 when he writes,

"Oh the depth of the riches of the wisdom and knowl-

edge of God!
How unsearchable His judgments, and His paths beyond tracing out!
Who has known the mind of the Lord? Or who has been His counselor?
Who has ever given to God, that God should repay Him?
For from Him and through Him and to Him are all things.
To Him be the glory forever! Amen."

In the Gospel of John, chapter 9, is recorded an incident which highlights the functional nature of crisis as orchestrated and facilitated by God. Jesus was walking along with his disciples when they came across a blind man. The disciples reacted by asking Jesus, *"Rabbi, who sinned, this man or his parents, that he was born blind?"* Christ's response is remarkably insightful and spiritually powerful, though, perhaps, not emotionally comforting. I quote Jesus: *"Neither this man nor his parents sinned, but this happened so that the work of God might be displayed in his life."* The rest of the story makes the point. Jesus proceeded to heal the blind man by having him wash in the pool of Siloam. His neighbors who had known of his blindness began to probe him for an explanation for his sight.

The news of his miracle created quite a stir in the community and provided Jesus the splendid opportunity to reveal Himself as the Messiah and to proclaim the gospel to many others. So in reality, the crisis that the blind man and his parents faced for many years was the very thing God used to bring into reality His very purpose for coming, to give spiritual sight to those dwelling in spiritual darkness.

The apostle, John, records for us yet another incident that depicts the functional perspective on crisis. Chapter 11 furnishes a story about the sickness and death of Lazarus. Mary and Martha, sisters of Lazarus, had sent word to Jesus of the serious sickness of Lazarus. Upon hearing of it Jesus calmly replied that, *"this sickness will not end in death. No, it is for God's glory so that God's son may be glorified through it."* Jesus loved this family greatly and had spent much time with them. But yet, he delayed for two more days. When he decided to visit Lazarus his disciples tried to stop him but he explained the necessity of such a visit. The disciples could not understand his decision to visit because he had told them Lazarus was asleep. Upon further questioning, he plainly declared to them that, *"Lazarus is dead, and for your sake I am glad I was not there, so that you may believe. But let us go to him."*

Upon arrival, Jesus discovered that Lazarus had been dead for four days. This was, of course, all intended and calculated by Jesus. His next step was incredible. After a theological discussion with Martha in which he declared the fact of Him being the resurrection and the life he sought out the place where they had buried Lazarus. A crowd of unbelievers followed Jesus to see what he would do. Then he prayed, *"Father, I thank you that you have heard me. I knew that you always hear me, but I said this for the benefit of the people standing here, that they may know that you sent me."* After this brief prayer, he commanded, in a loud voice, that Lazarus come out of the grave. The result was electrifying as the dead man arose and walked out. Many put their faith in Him while others plotted to kill Him.

It is to be noted that Jesus was primarily concerned about one thing: the glory of God so that people would come to know that he, Jesus, was sent by God to bring deliverance from the ultimate crisis, the prospect of eternal damnation and separation from God, the second death. We ought to note the frequency throughout the book of John, where Jesus affirms that his purpose was to honor God the Father in everything. God was able then and He is no less able today to use any crisis for His glory and for the salvation of His creation. The Christian who grasps the depth of this powerful truth will be able to weather any crisis no matter how insurmountable the crisis may be. Ideally, the internalization of the goals of wholeness and holiness as a mode of living equips the Christian to face any crisis and emerge even stronger than before the crisis. By this method of strengthening the Christian is better poised to optimize his life for the glory of God and the edification of those whose lives upon whom God is placing His mercy.

It should be understood that for all humans the initial response to the first major crisis in one's life is normatively dysfunctional. But time has a way of changing perspective so that sooner or later, if the person is seeking the will of God, he begins to perceive the functional perspective to crisis and actually experience joy as the Holy Spirit produces necessary spiritual fruit. The great King of ancient Israel, David, was a man whose life was marred by crisis after crisis many of which he had brought upon himself by engaging in behavior contrary to the will of God. In Psalm 119 verse 67, David informs us that, *"before I was afflicted I went astray, but now I obey your word."* In case anybody misses his message he gives us very unmistakable proof that his crises were actually for his benefit. In verse 71 of this psalm, he writes, *"It was good for me to be afflicted so that I might learn your decrees."* David speaks from the intense depth and vastness of his experiences. He understands as well as any human can possibly understand the pain of physical, emotional and spiritual crisis. What a remarkable conclusion after many years of suffering and complaining!

It would be wise for all Christian counselors and indeed all people to internalize the theology of suffering as exegeted from Hebrews 12:7-13. I quote, *"Endure hardship as discipline; God is treating you as sons. For what son is not disciplined by his father? If you are not disciplined (and everyone undergoes discipline), then you are illegitimate children and not true sons. Moreover, we have all had human fathers who disciplined us and we respected them for it. How much more should we submit to the Father of our spirits and live! Our fathers disciplined us for a little while as they thought best; but God disciplines us for our good, that we may share in His holiness. No discipline seems pleasant at the time, but painful. Later on, however, it produces a harvest of righteousness and peace for those who have been trained by it.*

Therefore, strengthen your feeble arms and weak knees. Make level paths for your feet so that the lame may not be disabled, but rather healed."

Scripture and personal experiences have a way of changing one's perspective on suffering and bringing it in alignment with God's perspective. With a divine perspective that which is negative can be viewed through different lenses so that what appears to be "bad" really becomes good. Many are familiar with the poem called, *"A Creed for Those Who Have Suffered"*, which crystallizes the functional perspective to crisis.

> *I asked God for strength, that I might achieve.*
> *I was made weak, that I might learn humbly to obey*
> *I asked for health, that I might do great things*
> *I was given infirmity that I might do better things.*
> *I asked for riches, that I might be happy.*
> *I was given poverty that I might be wise.*
> *I asked for power, that I might have the*
> *   praise of men.*
> *I was given weakness, that I might feel the*
> *   need for God.*
> *Almost despite myself, my unspoken*
> *   prayers were answered.*
> *I am, among men, most rightly blessed.*

The above scriptures and stories are powerful for counselors in helping crisis victims return to equilibrium. We note that God allows crises in the lives of Christians not as punishment, but rather as tools to help us grow towards holiness and become more effective witnesses of His kingdom. It is His hope that the crisis would not disable us but enable us to function at the optimal level. God does not desire that we go into severe disequilibrium but rather that we receive healing. Part of the healing is the right understanding of the crisis in terms of God's greater purpose in our lives.

Even with an initial dysfunctional response, it is God's will that we do not stay in disequilibrium but seek to learn His will and be restored to equilibrium. More importantly, He desires that we actually allow the crisis to move us to a higher level of spiritual maturity so that we may share in His holiness. Is such a hope on the part of God reasonable and possible? With God all things are possible! The wisdom of humans is foolishness with God. Whatever God purposes for humans is reasonable and possible. And His sovereign will is far more important and functional than our will. We humans make a choice; accept His will and become an instrument of His holiness and love or reject His will and face the ultimate crisis of eternal punishment.

Lessons from Apostle Paul

Let me now use two biblical illustrations to make the case for a functional perspective. I begin with the example of the Apostle, Paul in the New Testament. In **II Corinthians 12:7-10**, Paul writes: *To keep me from becoming conceited because of these surpassingly great revelations, there was given me a thorn in my flesh, a messenger of Satan, to torment me. Three times I pleaded with the Lord to take it away from me. But He said to me, "My grace is sufficient for you, for my power is made perfect in weakness." Therefore I will boast all the more gladly about my weaknesses, so that Christ's power may rest on me. That is why, for Christ's sake, I delight in weaknesses, in insults, in persecutions, in difficulties. For when I am weak, then I am strong."*

While Bible scholars still do not know the exact nature of this "thorn in the flesh" afflicting Paul, we all know that Paul suffered from a serious problem. The very fact that Paul pleaded with God for deliverance three times implies that this thorn was not just a little thing to be toyed with. One does not plead for deliverance when the discomforting situation is a small matter. Clearly, this thorn was a crisis event that could have thrown most people into a state of disequilibrium. It is likely that initially Paul might have responded to this crisis with some degree of emotional disequilibrium. He could not understand the reason for this crisis but as he spoke to God about it, God gave him a functional perspective.

Note that Paul records God as saying, *"My grace is sufficient for you, for my power is made perfect in weakness"*. Obviously, God knew things about Paul's temperament, personality, and spiritual condition that needed to be addressed in Paul's life so that he could become an even more effective instrument in His hands. Paul, himself, might not have been initially aware of these negatives which God recognized. God was very alert to Paul's weaknesses. It is apparent that Paul later became aware of a particular weakness, which God needed to correct. It should be noted that Paul acknowledges that

115

"to keep me from becoming conceited…." God permitted the thorn in the flesh.

I think that Paul is confessing a spiritual weakness of his, the tendency to become arrogant. Imagine the situation of a human being that is given the incredible honor of actually experiencing revelations from God. The first six verses imply that Paul was transported to the third heaven where God dwells and there he was able to hear, see and experience that which the average person will not experience. To have such an experience with the HOLY GOD of the Universe can indeed cause a human to become conceited and full of self. Any human full of self can no longer be a truly effective servant of God. For such a person would tend to take credit for himself when indeed it is God who deserves the credit. So what did God do to prevent Paul from this unhealthy feeling and consequent action? He afflicted him with a serious crisis in order that Paul would always have to stay focused on the power of God. God's knowledge, grace and love are far greater and far more loving than we humans realize. The dawning of such a remarkable truth upon the mind of Paul obviously changed his entire perspective on suffering, crisis and any other negative condition and facilitated Paul's usefulness as a vessel of Christ.

What matters to God is not man's aggrandizement. For mankind is not grand, big or really significant. God is big, grand and significant. So in order that humans not lose touch with the truth that God desires etched upon their minds He often allows a crisis. Paul came to understood this amazing truth and thus saw his several crises as things in which, and about which he could actually boast. Because by boasting about his crises, he could demonstrate the greatness and power of God. And all humans need to see, understand and experience the power of this God. Human weakness provides the ideal environment for the display of God's greatness and love.

What an amazing perspective when a suffering human in the midst of a major crisis event can calmly say, "For when I am weak then I am strong." Paul was acknowledging his own human frailty, his human impoverishment, his human inadequacies and dependency. To acknowledge such is to come before God empty and seek His grace as He chooses to give it to His servants.

A crisis that forces the victim to focus on God is indeed a very good thing. The real strength of a Christian comes not from physical strength, physical beauty, or perfect health. The person who accomplishes much by reason of his strength, beauty, health, money, fame, power or any other such earthly, fleeting quality will tend to not see and appreciate the grace and love of God. Thus real strength comes from an admission of one's weakness and one's acknowledgment of total dependency on the Creator who alone can equip us for the work of the kingdom. Thus we see how God's grace is sufficient for us because His power indeed is made perfect in human weakness.

The internalization of this perspective in a Christian who is experiencing a crisis changes everything. Suppose Henry who is a Christian is diagnosed with a malignant cancer and is given a very short time to live. This is a major crisis event. Henry can decide to respond as most people do; become despondent and despair of life, suffer bouts of depression and engage in self-destructive behavior. But the truth is he does not have to pursue such a morbid course of thinking, feeling and behaving. He can seek to understand God's greater purpose in his life and how this suffering can be to God's glory.

If Henry could find some way to use this crisis to glorify God and make Jesus more real to others who are suffering then the crisis is no longer a crisis. It is the work of God to magnify His name and build the kingdom of God. Thus Henry becomes a vital tool in God's hands as God works out His grander design for people by using the life of cancer victim, Henry.

Lessons from Job

I will now examine another case study, this time, from the Old Testament. Most Christians are very familiar with the book of Job. Here is a most fascinating story of a man who had everything that he could desire. Life was without doubt, a joyous and satisfying experience. He lacked for nothing. He would be the envy of most people who measure life in terms of material comforts. For Job, life was a lot more than material comforts. He was a religious man, too. In fact, the biblical account speaks of Job as, *"blameless and upright; he feared God and shunned evil."* Every day it was his custom to spend time early in the morning in devotions to God. For Job, it would have been unthinkable that a major, life-threatening crisis was about to occur.

Upon the instigation of Satan who challenged Job's faithfulness to God as simply a matter of expedience in terms of its functional benefits God granted Satan his evil request to destroy all of Job's wealth, smite his children with death and afflict Job with a horribly dreadful disease. As Job felt the impact of his unbearable suffering he cursed the day of his birth and would not be comforted. His three friends offered useless counsel in their efforts to convince Job of his sinfulness. They argued back and forth. Each offered his version of crisis counseling. The fact is that not one of the three provided any real therapeutic counsel of substance.

In other words, their crisis counseling to Job was a failure. They sought to explain his suffering by equating his crisis with his sinful condition and advised him to quit sinning. After much lengthy dialogue and debate they quit and then God Himself became the crisis Counselor.

The Eternal, Omnipotent and Most Holy God offered counsel that brought about a dramatic and remarkable transformation in Job's life. In fact, when God was finished counseling Job, his response to this amazing God manifests that he had experienced something most unusual and awesome.

I quote Job as he meekly replies to the Maker of the Universe: *"I know that you can do all things; no plan of yours can be thwarted. You asked, 'Who is this that obscures my counsel without knowledge?' Surely, I spoke of things I did not understand, things too wonderful for me to know. You said, 'Listen now and I will speak; I will question you, and you shall answer me.' My ears had heard of you but now my eyes have seen you. Therefore I despise myself and repent in dust and ashes.* (Job 42:1-6).

For the first time in Job's life, he had come to really know and experience in a very intimate way the power, goodness and holiness of the God he had been serving all his life in a very meticulously legalistic way. Job was without doubt a morally upright man; one whom even God spoke well of in His conversation with Satan. In fact, Job proved Satan wrong in his argument with God. But in spite of Job's moral uprightness, he had not yet come to the spiritual depth that God desired for Job.

It was necessary for Job to be further purified to remove any self righteousness, presumption, unholy attitudes and any other ingredient which God felt needed to be removed so that the Holy God could be totally glorified in Job's daily worship. Further, this incident serves as a cogent lesson for all humans of every nation, Christian or not, to know that ultimately, God and God alone is in control and we must submit to His will in our lives. Thus, even in our darkest moments of emotional and spiritual desperation God has not abandoned His children; He is simply purifying us to become optimal instruments for His purposes.

It would be shortsighted to not include the end of the story of Job. After his deep repentance God honored Job in a mighty way by restoring to him even more than he had before. In fact, the Bible says that, *"the Lord blessed the latter part of Job's life more than the first."* Thus God permitted in the life of a servant of His, a major crisis by which He could effect the attainment of positive spiritual objectives. Of course, not every crisis story ends exactly the same way. But then not everybody starts off as Job. Nor does God work with everyone in the same way.

The critical ingredient is that Christians need to place greater faith in God's sovereign will in their lives and respond in holiness as God works out His greater purpose. By adopting this methodology of thinking and functioning the Christian may turn a major crisis into a far greater blessing than he had ever dreamed of as possible. Without doubt, there is a functional perspective to crisis. It requires persevering faith, inexhaustible patience and persistent tenacity. God is still the good God and He will always be the good God even when we limited mortals are unable to see through the fog.

13: Implementation of Model

In this part I wish to examine the methods of implementation of this model for achieving the desired results. As with any plan or model the success of the plan depends on its ease of implementation, its efficacy, and the level of willing commitment to the discipline required to ensure success. Let me posit the view that a model may be very feasible and still not generate the expected results because people do accept it or commit to it.

Often, the discipline needed to guarantee success might be more than people are prepared to give. The greatest example of such is God's model for living the full abundant life. Unfortunately, many have never been exposed to it but many who are aware of it are not willing to really implement it because it demands a level of discipline that is not convenient or instantly gratifying.

Let me use a more mundane example: that of an athlete who may have aspirations of becoming an Olympic champion in the category of swimming. The coach draws up a training schedule that has worked successfully for hundreds of other swimmers. But, in this specific case, this athlete is not sufficiently motivated to practice for the numerous hours required daily for the entire training period. He is distracted by other cares and concerns, which negatively impact his training.

Tragically, he never meets the standards to make the team. The reason for his failure to achieve the aspired goal was not because the model was necessarily defective. Rather, he lacked the raw material as the base on which to build, or the adequate facilities in which to train or the consistent motivation and passionate dedication to reach the goal. Surely, he might have conceptualized the goal but failed to materialize it for lack of resources and discipline.

It is like the man who desires to be in the kingdom of God and enjoy eternal bliss but fails to accept the sacrifice of Jesus Christ as a covering for his sins. The door to the heaven is Jesus. There is no other way. With regard to minimizing or preventing crises there can be no magical wand to wave. In an age of instant gratification people desire instant cures so they break the laws of health and hope that some wonder pill would restore their health.

The fact is that the very order of creation does not allow for instant cures and instant growth. The infant cannot take a pill and suddenly become a teenager. The seed planted in the ground today cannot produce a ripe fruit tomorrow. Natural law as created by the Creator has ordained a course of growth and development for all things. God's purpose for humans cannot be purchased in a pill or a special medical formula, or the discovery of a new substance or an organ transplant.

It is common knowledge that habits are very difficult to break. So I am not naïve to believe that the majority of humans who study a book on crisis prevention or listen to a counselor are going to rectify their present course of thinking, feeling and behaving. Psychologists are well aware of the difficulties involved in unlearning especially after years of habituation.

Further, millions of people are very comfortable in their value system to which they have become attached and cannot understand why anybody should change their lifestyles. It is like the smoker who was constantly warned by his friends about the serious dangers of smoking and advised to quit the evil habit. They even provided him with an abundance of reading materials to prove their point. After four weeks of intense study the smoker returned to his friends and declared that, "I have read so much about smoking that I have decided to quit reading." This story is more real than funny.

Over the course of almost twenty years of working with thousands of people as a pastor and counselor I have come across far too many who have manifested no real desire to change their lifestyles, even though they were aware that their lifestyles were crisis prone. This book is not intended to address such people. The scope of such a problem is beyond the parameters of this presentation

I am focusing on those who would like to make their

lifestyles functionally wholesome and optimize their lives as servants of Jesus Christ. Such people need to be equipped with the knowledge, the dynamics and methodology of crisis minimization. But how is this vital information to be transmitted to generation after generation? I have a few suggestions that are workable on condition that people truly desire to optimize their lives for Christ. I do not intend to provide elaborate details. Educated counselors, dedicated pastors and other Christian leaders who are truly committed to the culture of wholeness and holiness should be able to fill in the details.

The Role of Parents

It is my belief that the institution of the family has the greatest power to educate the next generation to move away from the culture of crisis and death to the culture of wholeness and holiness. For too long Christian parents have allowed a secular society to educate their children in matters of critical significance. Parents for the most part have become too self-absorbed in their own pursuit of self-actualization that they are unavailable to their children. Thus millions of children are being reared by television, Internet and other forms of mass media that have become the tools of Satan to wreak havoc in the family.

It is time for Christian parents to reclaim their God-ordained role as the teachers and guides and guardians of their precious children. We cannot allow the mass media in the form of television, Internet, movies, popular books, popular music, secular magazines, and other such secular conduits to be the guides to our children.

The truth is that parents must begin to rebuild family life and not continue the abdication of this holy responsibility. In this matter of teaching children the path to wholesome living, we who are parents (I have three children of my own, ages 16, 12 and 8) cannot compromise with secular values if such values conflict with godly values. The Bible is our guide. We do not need secular authorities to teach us wholesomeness in living. Modern psychology is not a substitute for the instructions given by God. All of us who are parents need to wake up quickly before we lose our precious children to the culture of crisis and death.

If we parents are to reclaim our rightful roles then we must first become role models in our personal lifestyles. We cannot expect to model unhealthy habits and expect our children to develop healthy ones. So it behooves parents to develop and maintain a plan for nutritionally sound choices, regular exercise, daily personal devotions, frequent family discussions and spiritually sound living.

The point is really simple: If we want our children to be healthy physically, mentally, emotionally and spiritually then we must create the proper home environment to facilitate our children in achieving such goals. Therefore, Christian educators ought to establish appropriate training programs for all parents to learn the lifestyle of wholeness and holiness. In turn, parents need to set aside time to train their own children in the same way. The Bible admonishes parents to teach their children the right way and thus inculcate in them good habits for life.

The Role of the Church

It is alarming that many churches are places of unwholesomeness thereby contributing to the crisis situation. All pastors need to know, practice and teach the principles of wholeness and holiness. This is not to suggest that sermons become medical and psychological discourses. Sermons must consistently provide the required spiritual education to equip Christians to live the Christian lifestyle.

Additionally, since the Church is perceived as an institution of authority then it is quite feasible for churches to also make time for conducting seminars and workshops for educating their members in the lifestyle of wholeness and holiness. Special programs can be designed for the youths to equip them with the godly knowledge for wholesome living if we wish to spare them the horrible crises that many are doomed to experience by reason of lack of right knowledge.

Those who serve in the churches must come to understand the enormous power of the enemies of God. Today, it is fashionable and almost normative to perceive even homosexuality as a viable alternative lifestyle. In fact, some churches actually hire practicing homosexuals as clergymen. It is time for the churches to wake up and insist on the holiness of God in every dimension of living. The Church of God must not tolerate any lifestyle that is forbidden by God. The Church must accept all types of sinners, including homosexuals, to help move them from the culture of death to the culture of life.

Satan's plan is to infiltrate the very Church of God and use it for his evil purposes. No wonder that today some churches are actually contributing to the culture of crisis by permitting and condoning sinful lifestyles which God Himself condemns. Some churches simply reflect the darkness of this present evil system. They do not walk in the light of Jesus. They have borrowed from Satan's culture and in spite of what they may claim, they are no longer representing Jesus Christ as Savior and Lord.. God is warning such congregations: *"You have forsaken your first love. Remember the height from which you have fallen! Repent and do the things you did at first. If you do not repent, I will come to you and remove your lampstand from its place"* **(Rev. 2:4-5).**

The Role of Christian Schools

Within recent times more Christian schools are being established. This is commendable because it is certain that the public school system has become the nesting and resting ground of demonic forces to destroy our children and the family structure of this nation. . The Christian schools must therefore develop strong programs to combat the negative influences that surround us. Those entrusted with the responsibility to direct such schools should be targeting the urgent physical, emotional and spiritual concerns to prepare the leaders of tomorrow to avoid the crises, which those before have made.

Unless Christian educators are willing to defy conventional secular education then there will be no hope for the next generation of leaders. I would suggest that every Christian school have mandatory courses in preventive counseling, wholeness and holiness training, family health, Biblical history and Christian living.

Christian parents who cannot afford to send their children to private Christian schools need to closely monitor the school assignments given to their children and where appropriate meet with the school leaders to eliminate the trash that is being given to children as education. As a parent of three children all of whom are in the public school system I am very aware of these difficulties and challenges. I ask my children on a regular basis to inform me of anything that may be considered opposed to the teachings of the Holy Bible and Christianity in general. Of course, in this matter our power is very limited. But even so, we must do what we can humanly do and pray that God will do what His will is.

The Role of Christian Community Clubs

Christian counselors, pastors and parents should be

able to work together to form community clubs open to all people of any religious or political persuasion and use these clubs as forums to teach the lifestyle of wholeness and holiness. It would be advisable to establish women's groups, men's groups and youth groups. If these clubs plan their agenda well much good can be achieved as the benefits of wholesome living spread to the whole community. Healthy, social environments are necessary because people need social interaction.

Most of the entertainment and social opportunities available are crisis prone because they practice and encourage a lifestyle that will lead to crisis. Christian clubs must firmly reject profane values and promote godly values.

The Role of Christian Media

Media is power! Tragically those who control the media are agents of darkness. They are tools of Satan to create more dysfunction and disequilibrium within the society. One has only to look at the types of movies that are produced for public consumption and it is clearly evident that the media are anti-God, anti-Jesus, anti-Christian and anti-holiness.

Wherever one turns, especially in the big cities, we witness the attack against holiness and morality. The immorality abounds in magazines, books, videos, cable TV, porn shops, flesh markets, houses of sin and the Internet. Billions of dollars are spent by millions of consumers as they gobble up filth and seek even more in even more bizarre and perverted ways. Every year thousands of pornographic websites are added to the Internet.

Christian businessmen need to come together and secure a larger portion of the mass media market. Together working for the glory of Jesus we would be able to harness the diverse instruments of media, radio, television, magazines, Internet, books, plays, movies etc. to teach the lifestyle of wholeness and holiness.

With the combined resources of thousands of churches, Christian business leaders and the marketing power of media Christians can surely impact our society for crisis prevention and prepare more people for use in God's purpose.

14: Conclusion

By God's grace and good will, I have been blessed with this opportunity to study, research and write this book on crisis minimization and the maximization of our lives for the glory of God and His work on this earth. I am cognizant that this is just a small contribution to this enormous subject. It was not my intention to cover every aspect of crisis. Indeed, I could not do so even if I tried because crisis is a very multifaceted subject afflicting hundreds of millions of people on a worldwide scale. It was my intention to present a fairly comprehensive study that would get to the very core of the problem in order that anybody reading this material could find some help in the process of crisis prevention. More importantly, it is my prayer that you the reader would be able to use this information to maximize your life for the glory of God, crisis or not.

It is my personal conviction that as we journey through this new century, this new millennium, Satan and his demons would be even more busily engaged in his work of deception and destruction. It must never be forgotten that Satan is doing exactly what his nature is set to do. His job is to prevent people from entering into a holy relationship with God and to diminish the evangelistic effectiveness of those who do know Jesus Christ.

The Holy Bible clearly foretells that just before the end of this age and the return of Jesus the darkness of this world will intensify. Paul, writing to Timothy in II Tim. 3:1-5 warns us that, *"There will be terrible times in the last days. People will be lovers of themselves, lovers of money, boastful, proud, abusive, disobedient to parents, ungrateful, unholy, without love, unforgiving, slanderous, without self-control, brutal, not lovers of the good, treacherous, rash, conceited, lovers of pleasure rather than lovers of God – having a form of godliness but denying its power."*

My prayer and passion is that every counselor, every educator, every pastor, and every parent can become an instrument of change in this dysfunctional and sinful world. It requires that we who are honored by God to be leaders make a course correction in our own lifestyles before we can successfully impact the rest of mankind. The need for godly leadership is impressed upon us increasingly every day, as we become aware of the failure of society's long standing institutions. We are daily witnessing the tragic failure of man's wisdom as money, power, and carnal pleasures become the gods that the majority of humanity worship.

The Creator has been replaced by the creation as the object of worship. Such false gods offer short-lived delights with an apparent promise of eternal pleasure. But the reality is that these false gods have left behind a pathway littered with angry, frustrated, unfulfilled, broken people and millions of corpses who daily worshiped Satan without knowing it. And if we are to judge by the current obsession with the pursuit of pleasure and happiness then it is logical to predict that even more will become the victims of major crises because they are already on the road to major crises.

I offer this book as a little help in a major crisis affecting America, and indeed, the entire world. While I know that crisis will never be totally eliminated until the return of Jesus Christ, I am also aware that the decisions I make today will affect my life for the better or for the worse a few years from today. Therefore I must take responsibility for my life, my decisions, my course of action and the consequences of my lifestyle.

It is counterproductive to find someone to blame when my own actions have created the crisis event or crisis response. It is folly to blame the tobacco industry for your lung cancer. It is folly to blame the wineries in California for your liver problems. It is time that we learn to take responsibility for the lifestyle we choose.

I am also very cognizant of my Christian responsibility to help ease the burden and the heavy load that people carry. I am called to become an instrument of God's love and peace. So too is every servant of God. It is my conviction that if I do my little part in my little corner of the world then I can impact a few people to live more functional lives of wholeness and holiness.

They in turn would be able to impact multiple others and the process would continue to be multiplied. Surely if more Christians embark on a mission of mercy to assist others to develop a lifestyle that is guaranteed to effectively minimize or prevent crisis events and minimize dysfunctional responses to crisis events; then we would reach and save millions of people from current crises, future crises, and the worst possible crisis of all, the sentence to eternal death.

That we will create the utopia here on earth by our personal efforts to prevent and minimize crisis. Jesus Christ has commissioned His Church to go to the world and reconcile people to God. This reconciliation is only possible through the work of Jesus Christ. All who are reconciled to God are required to become lights in a world of darkness and corruption. If I commit to live according to God' laws then I will grow in wholeness and holiness and make a positive contribution in the lives of my children, my congregation and my friends.

Jesus came not to condemn the world but to save the world. I must become the love of Jesus on this earth until he returns to build His glorious kingdom. If millions of Christians begin to perceive their lives as the love of Jesus in action we can spare millions the horror of living in disequilibrium today and eternal anguish after the judgment.

Counselor or pastor or anybody, Christian or non-Christian can accurately predict the details of the future. Only God holds and knows the future. But I do have the freedom and the responsibility and the command from God to make the most of my life in the service of God. Every Christian has this same choice.

I pray that all who read this book may be motivated to make a difference first in your own life and your family and then for the benefit of humanity today and the salvation of many, for the future, when there will be no more crises of any type.

The apostle John writes of that future time of crisis free

living in which all will be completely whole and holy. *"Then I saw a new heaven and a new earth, for the first heaven and the first earth had passed away, and there was no longer any sea. I saw the holy city, the New Jerusalem, coming down out of heaven from God, prepared as a bride beautifully dressed for her husband. And I heard a loud voice from the throne saying, 'Now the dwelling of God is with men, and he will live with them. They will be his people, and God himself will be with them and be their God. He will wipe every tear from their eyes. There will be no more death or mourning or crying or pain, for the old order of things has passed away."* **(Revelation 21:1-4).**

May The Lord God Almighty hasten this glorious day! What a glorious day it will be when my glorified body will no longer be subject to any crisis ever again! Come Lord Jesus. Come Amen.

Endnotes

[i] Newsday Tuesday Dec. 15th 1998, p.B8

[ii] Ibid, p. B8

[iii] Judson Swihart, Gerald Richardson. *Counseling In Times Of Crisis*. Word Publishing 1987, p. 17.

[iv] Newsday, Sunday June 28th 1998, Dear Ann.

[v] Daily News; Wednesday March 1st 2000, p.16

[vi] Newsday; Friday November 13th 1998; Dear Ann

[vii] Dave Hunt & T. A. McMahon, *The Seduction of Christianity*, Harvest House Publishers, p. 8.

[viii] Douglas Groothuis, *Revealing The New Age Jesus*, InterVarsity Press, p. 16

[ix] Randy Reese & Frank Minirth, *Growing Into Wholeness*, Moody Press, Chicago, p.23.

[x] Richard Arno & Phyllis Arno, *Creation Therapy*, p.13.

[xi] Jethro Kloss, *Back to Eden*, (Back To Eden Books, Loma Linda, California) p. xxx.

[xii] Newsweek, Nov. 30th 1998, p. 62.

[xiii] Nutrition Action Health Letter, December 1998, p. 1.

[xiv] Ibid; p. 4.

[xv] Newsweek, Nov. 30th 1998, pp. 60-61

[xvi] Ibid, p. 61.

[xvii] Newsday, Tuesday December 8th 1998, p. A46

[xviii] William Duffy, *Sugar Blues*, Abacus Press, 1980, p.113

[xix] Newsday, Monday Jan. 4th 1999, *No Pain, Some Gain*, p. B6

[xx] Ibid., p. B6

[xxi] ICS School of Fitness and Nutrition, Study Unit 1, Scranton, PE., 1984, p. 17.

[xxii] Ibid., pp.17-18

[xxiii] Mary Vander Goot, *Healthy Emotions*, Baker Book House, 1987, p. 15.

[xxiv] Florence Littauer, *Your Personality Tree*, Word publishing, 1986, p.39

[xxv] Richard Arno & Phyllis Arno, *Creation Therapy*, 1993, p.1

[xxvi] S.I McMillen, *None Of These Diseases*, (Fleming H. Revell Company, New Jersey, 1979), pp. 64-65

[xxvii] Ronald M. Enroth, *Churches That Abuse*, Zondervan Publishing House, Michigan,1992, p.29

[xxviii] Newsday, Sunday Jan, 10 1999., *Israel's Other Y2K Issue*, p. A20

[xxix] Ibid., p. A22

[xxx] Newsday, Thursday Dec. 3rd 1998, p. A32

[xxxi] Ibid., p. A32

[xxxii] Newsday, Tuesday, November 24 1998

[xxxiii] Newsweek, January 17 2000. P.34

[xxxiv] Mark R. McMinn, *Cognitive Therapy Techniques in Christian Counseling*, Word Publishing, p.25

[xxxv] Richard J. Foster, *Prayer*, Harper, San Francisco, 1992, p.1

[xxxvi] Ibid., p.1

[xxxvii] *Diagnostic And Statistical Manual Of Mental Disorders*, Fourth Edition, American Psychiatric Association, Washington DC, 1995, p.327

[xxxviii] Internet, http://www.niaaa.nih.gov., November 1996

[xxxix] Newsday, Tuesday Jan. 12th 1999, Open Secret On Alcohol, p.C3.

[xl] Ibid., p.C3

(All scriptures have been quoted from the New International Version, published by Zondervan Publishing House, Grand Rapids, Michigan , 1995)

Denise
Dennis Griffin
Young Heart

For 8
news - 10p.